LEADING *the*
COMEBACK
CHURCH

Help Your Church
Rebound from Decline

DAVID F. NIXON

Beacon Hill Press of Kansas City
Kansas City, Missouri

Printed in the
United States of America

Cover Design: Ted Ferguson

Library of Congress Cataloging-in-Publication Data

Nixon, David F., 1946-
    Leading the comeback church : overcome the odds and rebound from church decline / David F. Nixon.
        p. cm.
    Includes bibliographical references.
    ISBN 0-8341-2102-6 (pbk.)
    1. Church growth. I. Title.
    BV652.25.N58 2004
    253—dc22

                                                                    2004001476

10 9 8 7 6 5 4 3 2 1

This book is dedicated
to my wife, Kaye, an overcomer
in her own right who generously gives,
unselfishly serves,
and lovingly supports
her comeback church pastor husband.

Contents

Foreword

In this excellent book, *Leading the Comeback Church,* David F. Nixon has captured the heart and story of most local churches. With a real sense of eloquence and no-holds-barred style, he expresses what most pastors deal with in difficult pastoral assignments.

It is with great pleasure and confidence that I recommend this book to the reader. I know David Nixon. I know his pastoral record. I know his journey with the churches that have been tough to lead. He is God's man, and his book reflects his passion and purpose in fulfilling the dream of building *His* church for *His* glory.

—Stan Toler
Author, speaker, pastor

Introduction

I'm a survivor. In 30 years of vocational ministry I have faced the ultimate test not once but six times. Six times I stood upon the threshold of defeat as I battled to save a church on the brink of death. God used me to influence these struggling churches back to vibrancy after major decline, crisis, or plateau.

Leading a comeback will be hard, challenging work. Such an assignment is not for the timid and weak but for those willing to embrace the challenge.

There are no quick-fix gimmicks to spur a declining church back to growth. However, I learned skills during my own experiences that I hope will empower you on your journey.

I pray that God will use this book to help you understand that He has called you to this challenge. The road you travel won't be easy, but God will use you to pour new life into your church and to bless your community.

1 It Only Takes a Spark

*A church cannot be turned around until a contingent of people is so
firmly committed to the ministry of the church that they will sacrifice
almost anything for the good of the church, to the glory of God.*
—George Barna

*The fire must be kept burning on the altar continuously;
it must not go out.*
—Lev. 6:13

The day before our 17th wedding anniversary, we arrived at our fifth
comeback assignment in a Midwestern city of approximately 190,000
people. Our reception at Lakeview Church was cordial, and the people
had learned in advance that it was our anniversary. They surprised us
with gifts. My first message was from Exod. 33:15, titled "Going with
God." In an attempt to set the direction for our ministry together, I declared that like Moses, we must find out where God was going and go
with Him. In essence Moses said, "An angel won't do! You alone must
go with us, Lord." I proclaimed what I believed: that God was ready to
go with us just as He had promised Moses (v. 14).

Lakeview was a strong, stable, but plateaued church with morning
worship attendance stuck on 265 for a decade, filling the sanctuary to
about 80-percent capacity. Ten years before, Lakeview had planned to
build a larger sanctuary on site but could not agree to break ground. The
church sat on a visible corner but had never permanently broken the
300 barrier.

With a strong vision for future growth, the church had purchased an
adjacent lot that included a former restaurant building and turned the
structure into its "Friendship Center," for fellowship and additional
classrooms. I inherited one staff member, the director of Lakeview's pre-
school and kindergarten. Our budget would allow for two others, so we
secured a youth minister, who also administered the buildings and

grounds, and a full-time minister of music. I began to cast a vision for growth from day one. Some thought I was pushing a little too hard.

One day Dan, one of the five retired preachers in the congregation, asked to take me to lunch. He had some fatherly advice to give. "Pastor," he said, "I like you and believe you're the man we need here at Lakeview, but"—he chuckled—"it won't happen by Thanksgiving." Just two months into the assignment and I was asked to slow down.

I saw great potential and I didn't want to settle back into the status quo, so when Dan told me to slow down, I reiterated my conviction: "I want our church to grow." I thanked him for the advice but knew I wouldn't be content in a holding pattern.

Gradually the people began to trust me to lead them. I began to understand that respect is earned one day at a time. For the first couple of years I chafed at the slow pace of progress.

No one step accounts for the way the church exploded with growth. Sometimes a spark is all that's needed to ignite the flame of growth. The people were ready. Their willingness became contagious. Once Lakeview broke the 300 barrier, they never looked back but continued to grow in the same building that had previously kept them from growing. Once the fire had started, my task was to keep fueling it. The following series of steps are what sparked and fueled growth off the plateau.

10 Steps for Leading a Church off the Plateau

1. Cast a compelling vision

I had been invited to attend a seminar on something known as the "K-Church Project." I knew only that "K" stood for 1,000; I did not know why a guy like me, pastoring a church of 250, had been invited until that afternoon seminar. I discovered that the K-Church Project was about vision. First I had to see the vision as a possibility. The very next Sunday I began to cast a vision that Lakeview could become a K church by the year 2000, even though our membership was presently less than 500. Before we could accomplish such a feat, I knew that some painstaking groundwork had to be done.

1988-89 became our "Year of Preparation." We spent this time

- Building relationships
- Training the pastoral staff
- Casting a vision for growth
- Enlivening the church's music and worship
- Soliciting prayer partners
- Developing a new membership manual
- Putting ministries in place that would facilitate growth
- Preaching and teaching on what it takes to be a growing church
- Changing the perception to "every member a minister."

On September 17, 1989, I began the service with an informal time of greeting and then turned the service over to Bill, my worship leader. I fully expected the music to begin, but Bill stepped forward and said, "Pastor, I feel like doing something different today."

What's going on? I wondered.

He then introduced Mel, representing the church board, who announced, "Today is Pastor Appreciation Day."

"Pastor," Mel said, "This is a day we have set aside to honor you. Dr. Roundtree is here to preach for you today. Sit back, relax, and enjoy the day we've planned."

My wife, Kaye, was escorted to the platform. After someone pinned a corsage on her, leaders from our church came to the microphone trumpeting the same message: "We're behind you, Pastor. We know the vision for growth that God has given you. We support you and are ready to pull together to see what God will do for us."

Hot tears of joy splashed the lenses of my glasses. Their actions this happy day told me they had been listening to my challenges for growth. I had earned their respect. Their love and loyalty told me that they were willing to follow my leadership. What I didn't know at the time was just how close we were to seeing our dreams become a reality.

2. Develop a concise mission statement

Our first order of business was to reformulate a clear, concise mission statement that could be easily memorized. Their existing mission statement was too long—47 words. I worked with my leadership to define our mission in 10 words: "Reaching people with the gospel of the Lord Jesus Christ." I did not try to impose my own statement upon the leaders. They worked together to hammer out a mission statement everyone could support.

3. Mobilize prayer partners

Next we mobilized the church to a vital prayer ministry, believing that the church moves forward only on its knees. Amazing things begin to happen when church members get serious about prayer.

We developed a prayer partner ministry and issued a challenge to the congregation. Forty-six people committed themselves to become my personal prayer partners. On each day of the month one or two persons lifted the pastor and staff to the Lord in prayer. On Sundays, two prayer partners prayed in my study during the services. Prior to the services, we joined hands, and they prayed for me.

I asked them to pray through the order of service, lifting up to the Lord each participant in the service. When the singers sang, they were lifted to God on wings of prayer. When the offering was taken, my partners prayed for the finances of the church. I felt energy to preach I had not felt in a long time. Our services were enlivened with the presence of God. Many were saved.

4. Develop a strategy for growth

● **Mobilize the laity for ministry.** With the prayer team in place, we began to concentrate on putting ministries in place that would facilitate growth in a deliberate attempt to mobilize the laity for ministry. We designed a membership manual, a kind of everything-you-wanted-to-know-about-Lakeview-even-before-you-asked compilation. The final part included a spiritual gift analysis based around the nine service gifts: evangelism, prophecy, teaching, exhortation/encouragement, pastoring/shepherding, showing mercy/compassion, serving/helping, giving, and leadership/administration. Gift definitions and scriptures were also included.

Next I painstakingly went through every ministry of the church and sought to match one of the nine service gifts to the ministry area. For instance, the gift of teaching qualified a person to teach a Sunday School class or Bible study group. The gift of mercy qualified a person to work in the compassionate ministries or care ministry. The gift of service qualified a person for any number of assignments based on a person's interest or passion. But what gift qualifies a musically talented person? If you have never taken time to list every available job in the church, do so.

Each new member identified his or her top three gifts and then was asked to give his or her top three choices for ministry. As each new class of members was received, these new members were asked publicly to make a commitment to ministry. When I introduced them to the congregation, I told what their spiritual gifts were and where they were currently ministering or sought placement as soon as an opening occurred. Over time, the congregation realized the importance of every member having a ministry.

● **Form a dream team.** A strategic planning committee began meeting weekly to dream, set goals, prioritize, and plan. This group, known as the "K-Vision Team," proposed that the following year be designated as our "Year of Expansion." The team began a strategic planning process to accommodate continued growth including new ministries, additional staff, facility needs, and the finances needed to fund the anticipated growth.

● **Expand facilities to accommodate growth.** In reviewing the history of Lakeview, we determined that we had been a "plateaued church" (plus or minus five-percent growth for at least five years) for nearly a decade. We set out to become a "break-out church" (five- to ten-percent growth for five consecutive years). Limited sanctuary space had contributed to the plateau, and an expansion project was undertaken to add 40 seats to the sanctuary, along with a new foyer and two additional classrooms.

● **Start multiple services.** The K-Project and my denomination's School of Large Church Management put me in contact with other innovative methods to double sanctuary space without going into a massive building project. John Vaughn, a church growth consultant, encouraged me to expand to two services as soon as possible. Then Elmer Towns drilled into my head, "You must be born again; you must be baptized; you must go to two services!" And so one week after dedicating the expanded facilities to God, we began an 8:00 A.M. worship service, effectively doubling our sanctuary seating accommodations without a million-dollar building campaign. Growth began, but not immediately.

• **Make reaching people the focus of your energy and efforts.** Having settled on a mission statement that might have been construed as rather simplistic, an overriding consensus developed in regard to evangelism. The K-Vision Team (strategic planning group) had been meeting weekly for more than six months before we all arrived at the same conclusion: Lakeview's number-one priority should be evangelism. The process of hammering out a mission statement had been tedious at times but well worth the effort. A growing church needs a focus that accurately reflects what the church is about. Lakeview's mission, "Reaching people with the gospel of the Lord Jesus Christ," became the focus of all our energy and efforts.

5. Trust God for the finances

I still remember the board meeting at which we agreed to make evangelism our top priority. I boldly challenged the board to approve the hiring of an additional staff member to serve as minister of evangelism. Somebody on the finance committee noted that we had not budgeted for an additional staff member, questioning the wisdom of such a bold move. But the more we discussed the need, the more convinced all became that this was what God wanted us to do.

God led us to contact a gifted personal evangelist with broad experience, and he was hired on faith that God would provide the funds to support him. When the leaders trusted God to supply the finances, income increased weekly to meet the need.

6. Focus attention on winning lost people. Try a "salvation candle."

One day in staff meeting we discussed the meaning of evangelism as Lakeview's top priority. However, we could not come to a consensus about implementing the evangelism thrust. But we did agree that something was needed to help focus our attention on reaching and winning people to Jesus.

After the meeting ended, I prepared to leave for lunch. When I walked into the hallway, Bill and Alex emerged from a hallway huddle and issued a challenge we'll never forget. Acting as spokesman, Bill said,

"Pastor, we think we should get a large candle and set it on a pedestal in the sanctuary. We'll call it the 'salvation candle.' Every time someone is saved, we'll light the candle."

I countered, "Won't that put a lot of pressure on us as a staff to see that it's lighted each week?"

"What would be wrong with that?" my staff said in unison.

Bill added, "If a week comes when the candle is out, it will remind us all that we have work to do."

• **Go public in your commitment to evangelism.** I had some initial doubts about the salvation candle but did not want to squelch my staff's enthusiasm, so I reluctantly agreed to go public with the leaders' commitment to evangelism. Inwardly I knew that now I had to get more personally involved in winning people to Jesus. We agreed that the candle would burn whenever anyone reported a person had prayed to receive Christ whether in a public service or in personal evangelism.

• **Leaders demonstrate faith.** As I thought about how to introduce the salvation candle to the congregation, the Lord directed me to Lev. 6, where two times it says, "The fire on the altar must be kept burning [continuously]; it must not go out" (6:12-13). The responsibility for the burnt offering rested directly on the shoulders of the Levitical priests. I knew that responsibility for keeping the evangelism fire burning rested on my staff and me. I seriously hoped I could light the candle during my message, introducing the idea on Sunday, but by Friday, as far as we knew, no one had been won to Christ.

• **Embrace the lost and the least.** We had been conducting our 8:00 A.M. services for several months. On her way to Sunday School one morning, Connie, mother of four, spotted a curious-looking man. He was pushing a grocery cart, half-full of cans, toward a beverage store across the highway. Instantly the Lord prompted Connie to turn around and invite that man to church. She dropped off the kids before heading to the liquor store's Dumpster. There she found George (not his real name) foraging through the Dumpster behind the liquor store. He was ill-shaven, weather-beaten, with the clothes and an odor to match.

Connie introduced herself and asked, "What's your name?"

"George," he said, expecting to be scolded for pilfering in the trash.

"Do you go to church anywhere?" Connie asked.

"No, ma'am—I don't," George said, his head dropping. "Who'd want me to attend their church?"

"We would," Connie said, her noticeably sweet perfume catching George's attention.

"You would?" George asked in disbelief. "Where do you go to church?" he said as his eyes brightened.

"Over there," Connie said pointing to Lakeview Church, just across the street on the corner.

"But I'm not dressed good," George protested.

"Come as you are, George—we take anybody," Connie said confidently. "In fact, the Lord told me to stop and invite you." She paused and then said, "Would you like to come today?"

"OK," George said to his newfound friend. "I'll meet you there in a few minutes."

Sure enough, George pushed his grocery cart across the four lanes of traffic on that busy corner while Connie waited at the front door.

• **Go ahead—light the candle.** Sunday morning came, and still no one had prayed to receive Christ. I admit that I worried that the impact of the message would be seriously affected if we couldn't light the candle on that first day. I went to the platform with Phil, ready to begin the morning service, but Alex was noticeably absent. Ten minutes into the service, he pushed open the back doors, his face brimming with excitement. He took a seat beside me on the platform and whispered, "Go ahead. Light the candle—we have our first convert!"

I asked who it was. "George. He just prayed to receive Christ in the classroom." Can you imagine the thrill of preaching my message introducing the salvation candle plan, then coming to the dramatic moment when I took a match and lit the candle—and then introducing George as our very first convert?

George got a few strange looks on his first Sunday at church, but he rarely missed a Sunday after that.

The staff initiated the candle idea, but all of us began to work to keep the fire burning. Early arrivers came to the sanctuary before going to class just to see if the candle was burning. From the first Sunday the candle was lit, a steady stream of new converts flowed into the church as a direct result of this effort. Eighteen months later, more than 90 people had been won to Christ.

• **Disciple new converts.** New converts had to be discipled, so people were trained to lead new Christians through a discipleship training course. For the first eight weeks following his or her prayer to receive Christ, each new believer received one-on-one time with a discipler.

• **Remember that salvation is more important than membership.** I periodically conducted membership seminars to prepare new people for joining the church. At one Saturday session, three women and a teenage boy were the only persons present for the class. As our *Welcome to the Church* video was showing, I heard sniffles and saw the women grabbing for tissues.

The video had several moving testimonies of people whose lives had been changed by Christ through the ministry of our denomination. These testimonies had so touched the women that they were moved to tears. When the video ended, I asked, "How many of you have ever prayed to receive Jesus Christ as your personal Savior?" Not one hand went up.

I realized that God had a different agenda for that morning. We reviewed the steps to salvation, and when I asked them if they wanted to receive Christ, all nodded affirmatively. Together we prayed the sinner's prayer. I followed up with scriptures of assurance and welcomed them to membership in the family of God. We laid aside the membership materials and signed them up for a more immediate need—discipleship.

• **Give your people meaningful handles.** Gradually the excitement for evangelism began to catch on with the people, not just with the paid professionals. Periodically we offered training to those who wanted simple tools with which to share their faith. The idea was to make witnessing a natural part of a daily lifestyle, not just a canned program. If you want your people to be involved in evangelism as a way of life, you must give them meaningful handles for sharing their faith. Equip them "for works of service" (Eph. 4:12), and don't be surprised if God gives multiple opportunities for your people to share their faith in their circles of influence.

7. Design special events for evangelism

• **Use national events for special emphasis.** Special events were used to heighten community awareness of Lakeview's presence and to reach out to people. The first year we had Firefighters' Appreciation Day. We invited the fire chief to come and received permission to send invitations to each of his firefighters. Not all responded, but enough did respond to make a meaningful event.

• **Become known as a church that cares.** During the Desert Storm campaign, we followed the news reports, especially of area men and women serving in harm's way. By making a few phone calls, we obtained the names of 50 local people who had loved ones in that brief war with Iraq. We planned a "Support the Troops" Sunday and invited the soldiers' families to be our guests. The prayer time was especially meaningful. The morning together climaxed with dinner provided by the great cooks of Lakeview. In a tangible way, Lakeview said, "We're a church who cares."

• **Heighten community awareness with media coverage.** By now we had developed a good relationship with the local television stations, and all we had to do was fax a news release to them informing them of special events. They usually responded by sending a camera crew and reporter. Many of the Desert Storm family members were interviewed and appeared on the 6:00 and 10:00 news that Sunday night.

8. Dare to care

A comeback church growing off the plateau must demonstrate its love for people in practical, loving deeds of kindness and mercy.

• **Support local mission efforts.** One year we invited the director of the local rescue mission to come and sent a bus to the mission to transport any residents who wanted to worship and eat with us. We chose Palm Sunday, and I preached a message on the triumphal entry of Christ titled "The Day of Decision." When I gave an invitation, five men from the mission responded, and our men gathered to pray with them. During that worship service over $4,000 was given for the support of the mission.

• **Give to help needy brothers and sisters.** The morning after Hurricane Andrew wreaked total devastation upon south Florida, my telephone rang early. A former member living in central Florida asked if Lakeview might want to take an offering to assist victims of Hurricane Andrew. I quickly agreed and passed the plates in both services that Sunday. By day's end I reported over $11,000 given in emergency relief.

• **Embrace real people with God-sized problems.** One afternoon my secretary put through a call from the director of our nearby crisis pregnancy center. She told me about a troubled young woman who had come to the center thinking she could obtain an abortion. Through counseling, they had convinced her to keep the baby and led her to accept Christ. Suzanne (not her real name) was a crack cocaine addict who supported her habit by selling her body on the streets of Fort Wayne. The director knew that she would need the nurturing support of a loving congregation to help her overcome her addictive behavior and prepare for the birth of her baby.

I promised to do what we could and telephoned Konny, a young mother I knew to be active in the pro-life cause. I had walked in peaceful pro-life demonstrations with her, and so I asked her to reach out to Suzanne. Konny made Suzanne's cause her own, nurturing, loving her unconditionally, encouraging her, and serving her other children along with her own family. Furniture and other items were donated for Suzanne's apartment. Konny organized one of the nicest baby showers the church had ever given. Miraculously, by the time the baby was born Suzanne was no longer addicted to cocaine. The church nurtured and supported her through her many ups and downs.

There is not a happy ending to Suzanne's story. One day she abandoned the kids a second time, and the children had to be placed in the care of extended family. Suzanne was on-again-off-again many times over the two-year period we reached out to her. One day she was gone for good, never to be heard from again. Caring laypeople invested a lot of time and money in Suzanne. Our only satisfaction was in knowing that Suzanne's children were rescued and placed with family who loved and cared for them in a safe environment.

We discovered the truth of Rick Warren's words in *The Purpose-Driven Church*: "If your church is serious about reaching the unchurched, you must be willing to put up with people who have a lot of problems. Fishing is often messy and smelly. Many churches want the fish they catch to be already scaled, gutted, cleaned, and cooked. That is why they never reach anyone."[1]

9. Start new classes to meet multiple needs

Consider classes for the physically and mentally challenged. One of the keys to growth was the start of new Bible Study classes in some cases for people with special needs. One couple had a physically and mentally challenged daughter impaired from birth. For years these parents had to rotate Sundays in order to participate in Bible Study and worship. The nurses in the congregation stepped forward to serve these folks with a care class for the physically and mentally challenged. Other families with children in need of special care brought them in their wheelchairs and received loving care so that their parents could receive ministry and a needed break.

10. Use music and drama to evangelize

• **Easter productions should have an evangelistic purpose.** During Holy Week, Lakeview's music department prepared a full production of *The Promise* with drama and music. Free tickets were made available to members to use in inviting people they were trying to reach for Christ. At first these productions were more performance-driven than evangelism-driven. Once evangelism became our number-one priority, even our productions were designed to reach people with the gospel. When our performances were evangelism-driven and bathed in fervent prayer, they became Spirit-anointed outreach.

• **A living nativity scene portrays the true meaning of Christmas.** Christmas week afforded us the opportunity to impact our community through a living nativity scene. Our very visible corner location was turned into the scenes of the first Christmas. A manger scene, a choir of angels, and live sheep provided people an opportunity to bring the whole family and tell the blessed story of Christmas. Fort Wayne is quite cold in the winter, so large numbers of people could be involved rotating in and out of the freezing weather.

If you cannot immediately implement all of these ten points, begin where you can, and plan for the future. Make sure you involve everyone of all age groups.

Even teens want a piece of the action! A young man, struggling to find his own identity, had a life-changing encounter with Jesus one summer. He set a personal goal of winning 24 of his friends to Christ when school resumed. In the first few months of the school year, he had already won 14. Talk about an exciting youth group! When teens get involved in winning their friends to Christ and see it happen, the youth group will never be the same.

Evangelism became the driving force of this comeback church. From the moment evangelism became its top priority, new life surged into a plateaued church. Since 1987, Lakeview has more than tripled in attendance and is now running more than 800 on Sunday mornings. In the fall of 2000 the congregation relocated to a beautiful new campus on 38 acres of property in a prime location. Evangelism continues to be the church's driving force.

2   The Real Deal

You have to know and accept the truth about yourself,
as painful as that may be, before you can achieve wholeness.
—Vincent Gallagher

Who am I, that I should go to Pharaoh and
bring the Israelites out of Egypt?
—Exod. 3:11

The well-intentioned pastor who does not understand his or her own psychological needs, shortcomings, and fears can create havoc. Most of my parishioners accepted the reality that I was not Superman, and they willingly forgave my mistakes and helped me overcome my weaknesses and problems. I don't know what the hypercritical would have done if I had refused to admit my own needs.

Moses' Burning Question

In his encounter at the burning bush, God told Moses that He had seen the misery of His people and had "come down to rescue them from the hand of the Egyptians and to bring them up out of that land into a good and spacious land" (Exod. 3:8). But when God asked Moses to join Him in this work of deliverance, Moses responded reluctantly, "Who am I, that I should go to Pharaoh and bring the Israelites out of Egypt?" (Exod. 3:11). Moses thought that the people would not believe him (Exod. 3:13). Generally we think Moses was experiencing a crisis of belief, but really he was just being honest about his strengths and limitations. Moses knew that he was not an orator but was "slow of speech and tongue" (Exod. 4:10). And even when he asked to be excused (Exod. 4:13), God refused to let this reluctant leader off the hook. His 40-year stint in the desert of Midian had prepared him to be a person of faith and action. In his desert exile, Moses had come to terms with himself. He was a work in progress. God wanted Moses for who he was, despite his reluctance. Perhaps the reluctant ones become the best leaders. A. W. Tozer thought so. He observed that the best leaders have no desire to lead. Like calling draftees into an army, God chooses men and women who are willing to give it a go.[1] Moses gave it a go because God had prepared him to be the deliverer of His people.

Self-Discovery

I wouldn't characterize my first ten years of pastoral service as comparable to Moses' desert experience, but honestly I was just about ready to quit. I needed something. About this time, I entered the doctor of ministry program at Drew University's theological school. Providentially, I chose to focus on pastoral care and counseling for my professional project, because I wanted to enhance my skills in helping the people God had called me to serve. My advisor from Care and Counseling, a local provider, agreed to become my advisor on the condition that I take Unit 1 of clinical pastoral education. This required six hours every Monday for 30 weeks on top of Drew's demanding doctor of ministry track.

Thus began a journey with a small group of fellow strugglers in pastoral ministry. The didactic sessions provided helpful insights about pastoral care and counseling, but the greatest dividend was self-discovery. One exercise required us to make a tape of one of our Sunday messages to be critiqued by the group. Another assignment required 20 verbatim written reports of our pastoral contacts and interventions, also evaluated by our peers. However, the weekly interpersonal relations sessions proved to be the most beneficial. James, our facilitator, seemed to know just what kinds of questions to ask to get us talking. Coming off a full day at our churches the day before, in these sessions we could talk about anything on our minds. I didn't think of this as group therapy, but I learned things about myself that otherwise I never may have known. In short, the clinical pastoral education experience gave me a new romance for ministry that sustained me for the next 20 years. It helped me answer the "Who am I?" question. Those who anticipate leading a congregation through the comeback experience must know the answer to this question. Considerable confusion exists about the role of clergy in today's society.

Clergy Role Confusion

Preaching, church administration, leadership in worship, and pastoral care demand a pastor's attention. But knowing yourself means having to come to terms with these conflicting demands and expectations. Who are you, really? You can't look to today's culture for an answer, because the secular, humanistic focus is often incompatible with our Christian faith. Clergy identity is further complicated by the fact that "clergy are no longer equipped with reliable, theoretical models of their craft."[2] Who you are as a person directly affects pastoral role and function. Success in functioning within the pastoral role seems to depend more upon *who you are* as a person than upon *what you do* in your pastoral role. Understanding who you are as a person, not simply as a professional, has a direct bearing on your ability to lead any church in a U-turn effort. You see, the most significant resource you bring to any local church is yourself. If you're blind to your own emotional needs, to your expectations of yourself and others, or to your rights and privileges in relationships, you'll probably be insensitive to these needs in the people you endeavor to lead.

A Healthy Sense of Self

The first step for attaining a healthy sense of self may be to recognize yourself as a person of worth. Each of us grew up developing a self-concept and sense of self-worth that had little to do with us and a whole lot to do with the hang-ups and problems of our parents and peers. I suppose that's why Paul Meier says, "All human beings have a certain amount of inferiority feelings."[3]

I certainly had my share. I grew up with bright red hair. Classmates teased me unmercifully: "I'd rather be dead than red on the head!" That gave me loads of self-confidence! One of my most painful memories of adolescence came at age 14. I remember asking a cute blonde-headed girl to sit with me during a Sunday morning church service. After the service, we were inching our way through the crowded foyer when *he* spotted me. With the voice of a bullhorn, Bob shouted above the noisy crowd, "Don't you know that red hair doesn't go with blonde hair?"

My self-esteem did a rapid meltdown. I excused myself and ran to the car sobbing. I had stopped crying by the time Mom and Dad got to the car, and I maintained my composure until we arrived home. When Dad turned off the car I bolted for my bedroom, slammed the door, and buried my face in my pillow. A few minutes later, Dad knocked on the door, anxious to know what on earth had happened. I blubbered out the details, reliving the pain of my shattered self-esteem. I'll never forget my father's reassuring words: "I like you just the way you are. You take care of yourself; you keep your hair clean and groomed. I wouldn't change one thing about you." That day my father wrote me a "certificate of worth." Reassured and feeling loved, I rose from that esteem-wrecking experience believing myself to be a person of worth. I can't remember whether the taunts stopped, but I do remember receiving a loving father's affirmation.

Write Yourself a Certificate of Worth

If no one has ever done so for you, you need to do what Paul Meier suggests in *Don't Let the Jerks Get the Best of You*: "Put a certificate of worth in your pocket . . . by developing a healthy, accurate self-concept." Dr. Meier asserts that three feelings work together like legs of a tripod to make up a person's self-concept: (1) Leg one is belongingness: feeling wanted and accepted, cared for, and enjoyed as a person. (2) Leg two is worthiness: the feeling we get when others in our lives approve of us and affirm us, making us feel we're OK. (3) Leg three is competence: the "I can" feeling of being able to face life and cope with its many complexities.[4] When you feel competent, you possess a "can do" attitude.

Some of us have to work hard to compensate for a lack of belongingness or worthiness by becoming as competent as we can possibly be. In the extreme this could lead to a false conclusion that *who we are* depends entirely upon *what we do*, our skills, abilities, talents, or what we've achieved. While most comeback efforts require 60 to 80 hours of work each week, that work should never be done to gain a sense of worth. We should expend our greatest effort accepting ourselves as God sees us. This is what Moses did—no more, no less. Warren W. Wiersbe is right: "God is as concerned about the servant as he is the service. If all he wanted to do was get the work done—turn a church around—He could send His angels, and they would do it better and faster. But He not only wants to do something *through* us, He also wants to do something *in* us."[5] You may need to get out of the fake-it-till-you-make-it mode. Get real and authentic by being yourself—your *best* self—and you'll be amazed at how God works in you and through you. My friend Harold Ivan Smith understands this. In a recent E-mail, he typed three short words that capture the essence of what I mean: "Be David today."

The Real Deal Pastor

With a certificate of worth neatly tucked in your pocket, let's look more closely at the personal qualities necessary to work in "the ill-defined realm of people transformation."[6] First, a comeback pastor needs flexibility, acceptance, gentleness, and sincerity. Next, add to these humility, stamina, obedience, and love. Ask yourself the following questions:

- Am I sensitive to human relationships?
- Do I possess a capacity for sympathy that's not overdone?
- Do I respect each individual, and am I willing to accept people as they are and not as I wish them to be?
- Do I understand myself and my emotional limitations and shortcomings?

If you answered yes to these, there's a good chance you have the essential qualities to lead a comeback church. To become a channel of grace to those we serve, we must possess these qualities if we expect people to share their concerns with us.

Believe me—successful comebacks don't just happen. In order to lead a church out of the humdrum of the past and into the glow of a vibrant future, a pastor must scrutinize his or her inner person, allow the Holy Spirit free rein in the heart, and not shirk from inner transformation. Once a leader's heart is turned around and a sense of worth ensues, he or she is free to begin developing the necessary qualities of the "real deal" pastor. These qualities include a capacity for authentic relationships, personal authenticity, personal autonomy, an allocentric attitude, and self-efficacy.

1. A Capacity for Authentic Relationships

How people come to know you as a person in your informal relationships determines whether they'll turn to you as their pastor with confidence. People tend to avoid the following:

- **The perfectionist,** who gives the impression that real Christians have no problems, shouldn't be surprised if no one turns to him or her for help.

- **The rigid authoritarian,** who sees only one side of every issue—his or her own—shouldn't be surprised if the telephone never rings.

- **The shallow impressionist,** who tries to dazzle people rather than minister to them, will not be allowed to minister except at some superficial level.

- **The ecclesiastical climber,** who views his or her present assignment simply as a stepping stone to a bigger and better assignment, shouldn't be surprised at the lack of in-depth relationships.

- **The preoccupied administrator,** who uses people to achieve successful church operations, may never know their deep personal concerns.

If your phone never rings and no one ever calls for an appointment to share his or her burdens and needs, there's usually an identifiable reason. Consider these:

- **Confidentiality.** If there's the slightest question about confidentiality, people would rather suffer quietly than risk candor. If most people lead lives of quiet desperation, there's without a doubt a broken heart in every pew.

- **Emotional immaturity.** Your own emotional immaturity may keep people from sharing their concerns with you. Beware whenever you hear people say, "I was afraid I would upset you." When we communicate that even small things upset us, our people will hesitate to share their concerns with us, caring more about our needs than theirs.

- **Busyness.** As you face the unrelenting demands of a U-turn effort, you might be tempted to communicate busyness. If you're insecure and struggle with low self-esteem, you may be unaware of the extent to which ministry meets your emotional needs. An easy way

to hook people into feeling sorry for us is to communicate busyness. Don't make the mistake I made of constantly telling your
people how busy you are. If you do, you need to be aware of why
you do so: communicating busyness is a defense mechanism to
cope with the irrepressible demands of ministry in our 24/7/365
vocation. The busier we appear to be, the fewer people tend to
overload us with their problems.

- **Quick assurances and easy advice.** If you really want to avoid serious involvement with your people and their concerns, you'll offer
  "blessed assurance" by applying the grace of a Band-Aid. Easy assurances are temporary, Band-Aid solutions to problems. These
  "pat-on-the-head" communications may spare you from in-depth
  work with the people God has called you to serve. Such commu-
  nicative maneuvers are perceived as a polite brush-off. When you
  think more about your own needs than the needs of others, you'll
  fail to give people the time involvement they may need.

I became aware of the "assurances and advice" plight in writing verbatim reports over the course of my 30-week unit of clinical pastoral education. Our advisor required us to write 20 of these, reporting what we
said and what the person with whom we communicated said in our var-
ied pastoral contacts. My written reports revealed a willingness to be
supportive, usually accompanied by an assurance of my prayers. When
confronted with the fact that I frequently used prayer as a polite brush-
off to avoid in-depth involvement with my people, I hastened to make
adjustments.

I discovered something else. I often used the "if" word in my communications. I caught myself saying, "If I can help you in any way, don't
hesitate to call." Then I wondered why no one called. You may do this
too. No matter how sincerely you say, "If I can help you, please call,"
such statements communicate disinterest and insecurity. To this day I
consciously avoid the word "if," substituting the word "when." That simple adjustment can make all the difference in the world in what we communicate. For example, saying, "When you need to talk, I'll be there,"
communicates care and concern and opens the door to ministry on a
deeper, more authentic level.

I cringe at funerals whenever I hear well-meaning mourners say ever so sincerely to the bereaved, "If you need anything, I mean anything, please call." I wonder if such words were ever said to you. Did you ever call that person for help? Why not? Perhaps you suspected he or she didn't really mean what was said. These pat-on-the-head communications may lessen your load, but they also block in-depth involvement and ministry to people where they really hurt. I still have to guard my words. Instead of offering to help *if* someone needs it—of course they need help—why not *do* some simple act of caring? You'll be amazed, as I was, at how simple acts of caring connect you with the people you're called to serve. For example, offer to arrange for meals so the grieving don't have to worry about how they'll eat when they need to. "Befuddle" the grieving person by doing a little more than what's expected or required.[7] Run an errand. If a grieving widow had no immediate family available, I often accompanied her to the funeral home to make arrangements. Another simple act of caring is offering to make phone calls. In these and so many other ways, I tried to be a "gimper" for the Lord.[8]

2. Personal Authenticity

The personal authenticity of the minister develops credibility and trust. Kouzes and Posner in their book *Credibility* offer this explanation: "Religious evangelists have been caught with their pants down, their hands in the collection box, and worse, the most sacred and spiritual traditions have been violated. People feel betrayed." In their view, this explains the current leadership "credibility recession."[9] Recent Gallup surveys indicate that barely half of the adult population has a great deal of confidence in the clergy. Four out of five adults say they expect clergy to live up to higher standards of behavior than they expect of other people.[10]

Climb the Leadership Ladder. In a world where religious beliefs are floundering, the pastor's authority is derived more from the substance of how he or she leads, the common understanding developed with the congregation, and from his or her authenticity in the roles of a pastor valued by his or her tradition. Those who achieve personal authenticity have reached the highest level of leadership—what John Maxwell calls "personhood." At this level, people follow the leader because they respect who the leader is and what he or she represents. Maxwell asserts that the climb to this level of relationship begins, however, on the lowest rung.

- **Position.** At this entry level, people follow you because they have to. Authority and power are afforded to you because of your title. People may follow you because after all, you're their pastor.
- **Permission.** At this next rung of the ladder people follow your leadership because of the relationship you have established. Now people are beginning to follow your leadership because they want to.
- **Production.** At this third rung on the ladder of leadership, people follow because of the way you produce, according to Maxwell. They appreciate the results—what you've done for the organization. At this level, people follow because of what you've done for the church. People like you and what you're doing.
- **People Development.** Maxwell's fourth rung has to do with reproduction. At this level people follow you because of what you've done for them. Both the organization and your people grow best at this level.
- **Personhood.** This highest level of leadership requires a long and difficult climb one step at a time up to this point. Only those who have been willing to pay the price reach this level. Those who are impatient never arrive there. Too many of us move on before we reach this highest level of leadership. The ladder to leadership is built upon authentic relationships, secured one step at a time. At this level people respect you and follow because of who they know you are and what you represent. Few seem to reach this highest level because of the time commitment required.[11]

Build a Strong Foundation of Trust. While many people may allow you to lead because of your position or job description, authentic leadership awaits those who will build a rock-solid relationship of trust.

History helps or hurts. Not much can happen in an organization until a foundation of trust is established. Prior disappointments and disillusionment with previous leaders often prolong the amount of time it takes to move to a high level of trust where ministry is shared. But unless a leader reaches this higher ground, the pastor and people face a tumultuous journey marked by hostility and mutual dissatisfaction. This may account for the frequency of pastoral changes; pastor and people never reach this deeper level of relationship.

Courtship. A helpful analogy for the pastoral relationship might be the process a couple goes through from courtship to marriage. A church may consider several pastoral candidates in the same way a person dates many people before the right one comes along. Before the proposal of marriage is ever made, a period of courtship occurs. When two people believe they love each other and are sufficiently compatible, the commitment to marriage develops. The wedding date is set. Preparations are made. Vows are exchanged. In terms of pastoral relationship, the "marriage" begins when pastor and people officially enter into a professional relationship. The church votes to call the pastor, or the bishop appoints, and a relationship begins.

A period of testing. Immediately upon the pastor's arrival at a new assignment, the people begin to test him or her. I felt this even as church members came to the parsonage to help unload the moving van and assist with the unpacking. They cautiously observed our moods and moves. They eagerly desired to give us respect because of our position, but they really didn't know us. They wanted to follow our leadership, but the extent of initial openness seemed to depend on the legacy of trust left by our predecessor. If there's a sizable balance in the bank of trust, a lengthy "honeymoon period" ensues. But if a deficit exists, a long, painstaking process of testing must be endured until there's a healthy balance in what Stephen R. Covey has aptly named "the Emotional Bank Account." [12]

Leadership is built upon a relationship of trust, one deposit at a time. No matter how much you believe that the position you hold demands respect, trust is established and maintained one thoughtful deed or act at a time. At times, I was too impatient, thinking, *I shouldn't have to prove anything to anyone.* After you've been at this a while, you tend to think you've paid your dues, and your track record speaks for itself. Really, all that your followers simply want to know is whether you're trustworthy. Trust is formed by your character and credibility observed over time. Leadership is built upon a solid foundation of trust. A credible reputation of trustworthiness is earned one day at a time. Whatever time is spent building a relationship of trust is well worth it.

The old Smith-Barney way. Before people willingly follow a leader's vision or act on a leader's initiative, they must trust their leader. Trust cannot be demanded—it's obtained the old fashioned way: we *earn* it. John C. Bowling in *Grace-Full Leadership* suggests that trust is earned and sustained through *consistency, dependability, and integrity.*[13] People want to know that their leader can be counted upon day in, day out. They want to know he or she will be there when it counts, ever ready to support and encourage. If there's the slightest hint of a lack in personal or organizational integrity, hope of a lasting relationship quickly dissipates.

When a foundation of trust is established, people feel safe with their leader. Only then do they invite him or her into a serious, professional relationship. If no one invites, nothing happens. If no doors are opened, no work can be done. When people begin to open doors and the leader earns credibility, the word spreads rapidly, and people begin to say, "We can trust him [her]."

Walk on the Leadership Higher Ground. There's a place of productivity and fruitfulness that's well within your reach. Go for it.

Where ministry is shared. Wonderful things begin to happen in a local church when a pastor and people reach the higher ground of leadership. The leader acknowledges that he or she cannot do all things well and begins to share the ministry. When we're willing to share, the laity will trust us a great deal more. Thus, they'll be more motivated to share the work and to honor our unique gifts.

Where creativity flowers. Good things happen when a pastor and people reach the higher ground of leadership. Your own creativity begins to flower. You'll find that vocational ministry is a life of joyful service. Your people may even support you in pursuit of advanced degrees.

Where the laity are mobilized. When a pastor and people walk on this higher ground, each person is empowered to use his or her unique gifts and abilities to accomplish the mission and goals of the organization. In turn, still others are mobilized to work toward mutually shared goals. Only those who are willing to empower others will reach this stage of shared ministry. Your people need to be liberated to do that for which they're uniquely gifted. When we ennoble people to ministry, each Sunday School class or committee will reflect the positive thrust. Pastor, you must take the chains off and let them help you meet the irrepressible demands of ministry. Practice clean delegation, giving responsibility and the appropriate authority to act, and your people will begin to believe genuinely that they can make a difference. Your willingness inspires them to go places they would never go on their own and to attempt things they never thought were possible.

3. Personal Autonomy

A third quality of the comeback pastor involves several vital directives.

Have Self-discipline. Personal autonomy has to do with the inner ability to govern yourself. This requires a strong measure of self-discipline or the ability to call yourself to constant accountability. As Lanson Ross said in a seminar, "God is not honored by our lives being out of control."

Not noisy self-assertion. You may think because you're highly trained and are the resident paid professional that you're most qualified to determine what's best in all aspects of church life and business. This might be true, but you dare not communicate that you feel you're always right or even that you're usually right. This condescending attitude smacks of authoritarianism. Autocratic statements like "This is the way it will be" have a negative impact on the morale of any organization. Nobody is right 99.9 percent of the time on every issue. Autonomy doesn't mean that.

The ability to maintain balance. Autonomy is the capacity to balance and resolve opposing demands within you and between you and the congregation. This ability has to do with balancing your values and intelligent self-interest with the interests of the congregation you serve. Such a capacity implies not power over members but power *shared* with members.

A facilitator, not a dictator. A wise leader does not surprise his or her people with edicts from above but allows those to whom jobs are delegated decide how they'll be accomplished. Such a leader is out not to guard his or her own interests but rather to serve the interests of others.

Avoid What Is Inappropriate. The capacity for personal autonomy is usually learned by mistakes in our responses to criticism, blatant defensiveness, or questionable reactions. If your own needs get in the way of hearing the needs and concerns being expressed—at times communicated through criticism—you've not yet learned to be autonomous. Every criticism contains a measure of truth. We must train ourselves to look for that kernel of truth rather than react negatively to the criticism. When we focus on reacting to the criticism, we may miss what the person is revealing about himself or herself and will respond by condemning, pacifying, or patronizing our critics.

Care Enough to Confront. Only leaders who have the capacity to be autonomous can successfully cope in the climate in which pastoral ministry must be conducted today, particularly in churches in need of a major turn-around. This need to be self-governing (not just to be free to do your own thing), to be autonomous, to stand on your own feet is an essential quality if there are to be authentic relationships in the local church. Properly understood, personal autonomy enables the leader to introduce or sustain anxiety in church life in order that spiritual growth may occur—yes, even to temporarily get on bad terms with others if necessary for the sake of the growth of all your people.

Many pastors refuse to risk confrontation for fear of conflict and because of their need to be liked by everyone. This is scary when sin needs to be confronted, and yet, to avoid a conflict, they look the other way for fear of a blow-up. At the heart of this fear is the belief that the person might leave the church. Frankly, some of us are totally hamstrung in doing what our people need because of our unacknowledged need to keep people tied to the church. We allow our desire to keep everything running smoothly to take precedence over risking confrontation that might result in growth and healing for everyone involved. This is particularly true in denominations in which the congregation periodically votes on whether to retain its pastor. If you face a recall vote, confrontational risks are usually avoided until you know you've survived the vote or the periodic review of pastoral relations.

Choose your issues. Some issues are not worth fighting over. Hans Finzel in *The Top Ten Mistakes Leaders Make* gives an important piece of advice: "Draw your lines in the sand where it counts."[14] When I've had to confront, I've tried to wait patiently for an appropriate time to confront the people who need correction. This waiting period involves ample prayer. At times I've found that God will providentially open up an opportunity for me to facilitate the necessary confrontation. Remember: running headlong into a confrontation is usually not God's idea of perfect timing.

THE DESA APPROACH TO CONFRONTATION

A helpful approach to confrontation that I learned in a seminar once and that I have used many times is called "the DESA approach" to expressing yourself sincerely. I typed the acrostic on a card for quick reference at times when I have to confront an issue:

- **Describe** the other person's behavior objectively, avoiding an emotional response. Use statements like "I've noticed . . ." to describe his or her behavior in concrete terms, giving specific time, place, or frequency of action. Always describe the action, and never attempt to guess at the person's motive.

- **Express** your thoughts and reactions to the other person's behavior (how it makes you feel). Do this as calmly as you can to avoid an emotional outburst. State your thoughts in a positive manner without resorting to put-downs or attack. Stay focused on the offending behavior you observed. Never attack the person's character. Try to express yourself using a statement like "This gives me the impression . . ."

- **State** specifically what you want the person to do. There is, of course, no guarantee that he or she will do what you ask, but go ahead and ask for some small change. At the most, ask for one or two changes at a time. Take into account the person's capability to make these changes and his or her needs. Specify what you're willing to do to make the change work.

- **Aim** toward reaching a cooperative, mutually beneficial agreement. Carefully review the good and bad consequences as well as rewards and penalties. The use of "What if" statements can be helpful. Allow the other person the freedom to make a willful commitment to change. If the person happens to be a staff member, you might want to follow up with an agreement in writing.

An autonomous pastor cares enough to confront even at the risk of being misunderstood, because such a pastor cares about the growth and development of the people he or she serves. Those who refuse to confront may have superficial peace, but it comes at the expense of authentic relationships built on truth-telling.

4. Maintain an Allocentric Attitude

Most pastors don't concern themselves with psychoanalysis, but we would do well to develop the *allocentric* attitude in all our relationships. Allocentricity refers to the analyst's capacity to become interested in the totality of any object (person) without interference from his or her own needs. Simply put, pastors must put the needs of others first. Authors Kouzes and Posner state in *Credibility,* "Leaders must have the interests of others in mind first, rather than personal objectives. Leaders who are clearly interested in their own agendas, advancement, and well being (first), are not willingly followed."[15]

Three issues seem to hinder the pastor's ability to put others first without interference from his or her own needs: self-awareness, self-denial, and self-absorption.

Self-awareness has to do with the level and extent to which you're aware of yourself, your feelings, and your values. Below are a few questions I would like you to ponder as this chapter closes. I'll spend a little more time on the first than the other questions, because it's so important to the "real deal" pastor.

1. *Do you feel that more commitment is demanded of you than is practiced by the people you serve?* The pastor is frequently torn between his or her commitment to the church and his or her own personal and familial needs. You may be tempted to think that the laity don't commit themselves to the extent that you do. I've laid my share of guilt trips on committed laypeople, especially in my early years as a vocational minister, often without knowing I was doing so. At times I made them feel that nothing they did was ever enough. They might attend every single church service and extracurricular activity, tithe, teach, and pledge to faith promise, and the minute they miss one hot dog roast, they're looked down upon. This is what many devout laypeople feel. I know, because they've told me so.

Presently I know of one church where the dedicated laypeople are essentially suffering in silence. The only reason the pastor hasn't been run off is because, frankly, the board members are more dedicated to biblical conduct and to living Christ than he is. They don't want to do anything unchristlike, so they're hanging in there in desperate silence until he decides to leave. In the process, they give him nice birthday gifts and bonuses and graciously bend to his needs. All the while, they're discouraged with his leadership—but they don't want to hurt him, so they continue to do their best to support him as they feel a good board and church should. The pastor is clueless to the hidden desperation.

Few pastors know that this sort of thing goes on, because dedicated laypeople don't talk about it much with the leadership. What the leadership hears is usually just petty gripes from laity who aren't as sold out to Jesus. Those really trying to live Christ aren't going to gossip or spread dissension. I've been told that there's a silent communication among consecrated laypeople that pastors never hear. At times, they have been made to feel that the only way to please their pastors is to pitch a tent in the sanctuary and never leave. All this is to say that pastors can have misplaced expectations just as laypeople do when they expect too much of their pastors. The more we focus on our people's shortcomings, the more likely they are to pull away.

If our people's dedication is declining, perhaps there are real underlying reasons that should be addressed. For instance, if a couple is going through a serious crisis, the wise pastor doesn't automatically jump to the conclusion that their spiritual walk and dedication to the church are declining—especially if they've oozed dedication in the past. Instead, he or she says, "Are you hurting? How can I help?" and avoids unnecessary confrontation, conflict, and misplaced expectations—and also avoids wounding the very people he or she is supposed to be leading. Don't jump to conclusions. Show mercy. Give a little more grace. Hold your people up in prayer, and support them with love.

Some misguided pastors tend to track the giving records a little too closely. One pastor took a ministry student into his study and berated him for not paying his tithe. The pastor had been scrutinizing the church giving records and had realized that Bob (not his real name) had quit tithing. What the pastor didn't know was that Bob had lost his job and had no income to tithe. He was essentially struggling with being able to buy food to eat. Do you know what Bob did? He sat in that study and listened to what the pastor said and didn't say a word. He calmly let his pastor finish, walked out, and never returned to the church. I'm sure the pastor thought, *I told him, and he didn't like the truth, so he left.* The pastor thought his tirade was corrective when he essentially was responsible for Bob's leaving the fellowship.

Unfortunately, there's often a "them and us" mentality that pastors have toward laypeople. Such an attitude builds walls instead of bridges. It isolates. In healthy, authentic relationships there's no "them-us" mentality. Instead, there's a spirit of *we're all in this together.* No walls. No looking down on the laity. So walk the higher ground of authentic relationship based on mutual respect, and an artesian well of trust will always be present to draw from.

2. *Do you do what you do out of a sense of duty more than delight?* If so, vocational ministry has become an increasing burden and drain upon your emotional resources. Sure, ministry can feel like the hardest work in the world; but in many ways, it's the happiest work in the world. For it to remain a delight over the long haul, you must find your greatest joy in serving Jesus. Wiersbe poses penetrating questions that only you can answer: "What would you do if God took your ministry away from you? Would you be relieved and start looking for something else to do? If so, it's possible you shouldn't be ministering in the first place." Would you calmly drop out of the race, become bitter, and turn your back on the Lord? Or would you seek His face and plead for the privilege of serving Him?[16] The remedy is to keep your focus on the privilege granted to you and on the joy of serving Christ.

3. *How well do you respond to the criticism you receive?* Have you become so sensitive to criticism that the slightest affront haunts you for days and affects your wholesome response in other relationships in the parish? Do you ever fall victim of the criticism trap? If so, perhaps you'll find yourself running errands to please and placate your people rather than taking care of true ministry needs or caring for your family or even your own legitimate needs. The remedy is to look for the kernel of truth

in the criticism. Forget about absolute perfection. Model growth instead. Capitalize on your strengths; compensate for your weaknesses.

Self-denial has to do with the extent or level that you fail to take care of yourself and your own needs. Most pastors desire to be significantly involved in the lives of their people. But do you sometimes feel that this is more of a liability than an asset? Could it be that you're too available to your people? A person inattentive to his or her own needs would be available 24/7/365, never taking care to replenish or rejuvenate or recreate. The remedy is not to refuse every interruption that disrupts your otherwise orderly life. Interruptions are the stuff of which ministry is made. When the telephone jolts you awake in the middle of the night, taking care of your own needs doesn't mean you refuse to help because you need your rest. But learn to screen the frivolous. If your holiday or day off is interrupted, take comp times another day. The problems come when you're so consumed by meeting the needs of others that you neglect your own needs. Balance is the key.

Self-absorption is a tendency to be preoccupied with your own needs, desires, and interests, which prevents allocentricity. For me, this became apparent in my life by my over-investment in "membership" concerns.

Initially in the comeback efforts I led, more people were leaving the church than were coming into it. I blamed myself and tried to keep them tied to the church rather than hearing what they were saying about the church and their own needs.

For too long I tied my sense of success to the number of people I managed to reach and keep in church. My need to be successful caused me to offer assurance to persons with impossible problems, Band-Aid solutions to longstanding and insidious conflicts, and guilt-ridden injunctions regarding church attendance and participation. At the time I didn't realize that my keeping a tally and basing my worth on the congregational numbers and statistics reflected a measure of self-absorption that suggested that I was in ministry for myself. Only when I based my worth on who I was in Christ rather than on what my peers thought of me or on the size of the church did I experience the freedom to radically impact my churches for Jesus Christ in a way that empowered a breathtaking U-turn. I stopped ministering with the awareness of how I looked and started ministering with a God focus. I stopped offering placation and started being real with my people in a way that freed them to be real with me and freed us to both be real before the Lord.

5. Practice Self-efficacy

When I learned about the allocentric attitude, I discovered that I could serve people with complete openness. This allowed me to be more fully engaged with my people, serving with a greater sense of self-confidence or self-efficacy. The greater your sense of self-efficacy, the less stress and depression you feel in difficult situations. The higher your self-efficacy, the more capable of leading a comeback church challenge you may be.

I began this chapter with the candid admission that my own self-discovery did not occur until I had been at ministry for ten years. You don't have to take that long. Try these steps to personal authenticity:

1. **Let God affirm your worth as a person.** Write yourself a certificate of worth. You're wanted, accepted, and enjoyed as a person by those who know you and by the Lord you serve. Be your best self.

2. **Honestly examine yourself.** Review the essential personal qualities I wrote about earlier in this chapter. Do you have some doubts? Test your answers by asking a trusted colleague or friend to be honest with you. What you don't know about yourself *can* hurt you. Ignorance is not bliss.

3. **Change what you can.** Admit your shortcomings, failures, and mistakes. If you've been too much of a perfectionist or too authoritarian and preoccupied, ask God to change you. Quit doing what's ineffective and unproductive. You cannot achieve instant emotional maturity, but you can confess your need and ask God to help you grow and develop into the most useful servant you can be.

4. **Practice proven leadership principles.** The climb from leadership by position to leadership by personhood takes time. A relationship of trust is built one positive step at a time. Your consistency, dependability, and personal integrity will build trust over time and will lead you and your people to the higher ground in leadership.

5. **Exercise personal autonomy.** This is not to be confused with self-assertion or authoritarianism. Become a facilitator. Avoid defensive-

ness. Respond appropriately to criticism. Care enough to confront, even if it means temporarily getting on bad terms with those who need correction so that growth and healing can occur.

6. **Open your eyes to the real you.** You can't go far if you're blind to your true self. Ask the Holy Spirit to reveal how others perceive your words, attitudes, and actions. Own what the Spirit reveals to you. You may need guidance through this process—as I did. If so, seek a counselor or a same-gender accountability partner or group. Remember—you have needs too. Avoid extremes in self-awareness, self-denial, or self-absorption, and you're on your way to becoming a real deal pastor.

"Who am I?" Moses asked. God must help you answer this question. He has confidence in you. Perhaps He saw something in you that others did not see. The Lord believes you have what it takes to be His servant in this difficult and demanding place.

3   No Woe, Don't Go!

Ministry is not just another way of making a living;
it's a wonderful opportunity for making a life,
a life that's lived for others.
— Warren W. Wiersbe

Have I not commanded you? Be strong and courageous.
Do not be terrified; do not be discouraged, for the LORD your God
will be with you wherever you go.
—Josh. 1:9

Charles Haddon Spurgeon (1834-1892) was called to Park Street Church in London when he was 19. He began preaching in a 1,500-seat sanctuary with fewer than 200 people attending. Nine years later, the Metropolitan Tabernacle was built to accommodate the thousands of people who flocked to hear him preach. During his 30 years of pastoring, his congregation included 6,000 regular worshipers and 14,000 members. Spurgeon pastored one of the most influential churches of the 19th century. He counseled young men to avoid the ministry "unless they felt irresistibly compelled, certain of God"—to be outstanding laypeople but not to enter vocational ministry without a divine call.

Oswald Chambers (1874-1917) trained for a time in college in the field of art, but when door after door refused to open to a career in that field, he began to feel an inner stirring to become a minister. He pondered, *Could God be leading me in that direction?* He knew he would have to abandon his art studies and leave the university. Most significantly, he would exchange a life work uniquely suited to his interests and gifts for something to which he had never aspired. In a letter to George Oxer he wrote, "I shall never go into the ministry until God takes me by the scruff of the neck and throws me in." As it turned out, Chambers found no peace until he did the thing God called him to do. Neither will you until you accept God's call.

At times it can be easier to accept the general call to ministry than to accept the difficult and specific task of turning around a whole congregation. All of us would love to take the church that's already thriving and continue in the wake of previous success. But those assignments are often nothing more than fantasies that only heighten our sense of despair when faced with the stress of leading the comeback challenge.

My Own Journey

I first heard God's invitation to ministry at a junior high school camp in the summer of 1961. As I sat with friends near the back of the tabernacle on our campground near White Springs, Florida, God began to move on my heart. I can't remember the Scripture the evangelist used, but I distinctly remember being drawn to an altar of prayer at invitation time. Prior to that time, whenever I needed to confess some sin—almost weekly as I recall—I would go forward to pray. This time, at camp, I felt a strange compulsion to go forward but without any sense of condemnation. The Holy Spirit drew me forward, and I stepped out.

I knelt to pray, waiting, listening. Before a word could form on my lips, God spoke to me in what seemed like an audible voice. I looked around to see if anyone else had heard the voice. No, the other teens were deeply engrossed in their own prayers. There and then, God singled me out, saying, *David, follow Me into full-time Christian service.* I didn't protest with "Can we discuss this?" Instead, *Yes* seemed to be the only appropriate response. On that hot summer night in Florida, God assured me that He had something special in mind for my life.

I hadn't arrived home before the doubts began. Being 14 and ready to get on with my life, I needed assurance. *Is this really what God wants me to do?* I determined I would find a Scripture verse upon which to base my call. Locked securely in the hallway bathroom, I closed my eyes and twice opened my Bible, using the old let-your-finger-fall-on-a-promise routine. Both attempts failed to give me the confirming proof I needed. My emotions ranged somewhere between silly and serious. I finally said, *OK, Lord. I'm not exactly sure what You want me to do, but I'm willing. Make this call something I can never get away from, and I'll pursue it.* God took me up on my willingness, and now, decades later, His call still compels me.

From the moment I said yes to God's will and plan, I've had a direction in my life that I could never get away from. However, I'm sure God must have wondered himself if I would survive my volatile teenage years. But I did. And once I settled God's will for me, I knew that if I ever hoped to achieve the highest and best life had to offer me, I had to preach. I went to college and seminary to prepare myself to do just that. In each comeback church I've pastored, through the highs and lows of this vocation, a bone-deep sense of divine call to ministry has been the one constant that has kept me in ministry. My call has given me validity, legitimacy, fulfillment, and authority throughout three decades of vocational ministry.

When All Else Fails

The inner call of God is a stabilizing, energizing, self-motivating force that will compel you to go on when every external motivation is removed and circumstances seem to warrant defeat. Thank God for the encouragement to proceed even when we think we can't. The Lord's servant who accepts His call can lean on Him and move forward with the poise of God's presence.

One of my tasks as a leader in the denomination I serve is to install new pastors on their first Sunday at what we call a "covenant service." I remind congregations that the call of the pastor is not in the hands of the search committee, the church board, or even the denominational leader, although each one plays a part in the selection process. The call is God's doing, not ours. "In John Wesley's terms, accepting the call means to be 'ready to do anything, to lose anything, to suffer anything.'"[1] This is why I say, "No woe, don't go."

At times, my commitment to God and to vocational ministry have borne the strain of leadership. Stretched beyond natural limits, my faith persevered because I had settled the matter of my call. There are built-in pressures that go with a comeback church assignment that only a God-given call can withstand. When every external motivation to proceed is removed, vocational ministers must see themselves as under a bone-deep sense of divine call to ministry. This sense of divine call is a steadying influence for turbulent times. Without this heavenly vision, many more will leave the ministry to alleviate the pressure. Even beleaguered servants will find peace in the midst of the storm when they remember that God sent them out as a "sheep in the midst of wolves" (Matt. 10:16, KJV). The memory and recurring call to vocational ministry will keep you going during difficult and trying times, as well as during the challenging and exhilarating ones.

There will be days of uncertainty and inadequacy. Some days you will have more questions than answers. Haunting questions like "What's a nice guy like me doing in a place like this?" You'll give until it hurts. Your well will be running dry. Or some homegrown hypocrite levels a criticism that sticks like Velcro to your wounded spirit. I've been there, and so have you. I can tell you that when every external motivation has fallen away, God's call is the internal and eternal motivation to keep you going. When you're called upon to face the demonic stirrings in congregational life and you find yourself wrestling against the powers and strategies of hell, the One who called you will be there to see you through.

This deep sense of call has kept me going all this time. Like the Eveready bunny, I'm still going and going and going—because God continues to provide direction and inner strength when extreme pressure flattens me on the floor and I have nothing more to give.

Long hours of work and unending demands hold open the doors of discontent. Admittedly, we're in one of the lowest-paid professions, requiring more education than we can afford, and we're expected to do every imaginable task. Critics may sneer that vocational ministry is a "curious hangover from a bygone era" and that we who respond to God's invitation are pouring our lives down an ecclesiastical rat hole. But Vernon Grounds is right: "Vocational ministry is still the world's greatest job."[2] I never want to join the ranks of those spiritual casualties who become disobedient to the heavenly vision.

God's Special Assignment for You

Those who give themselves to special assignments do not *choose* to serve; they *respond* to God's invitation. Just as God issued my call to ministry and empowered Spurgeon, so He still issues the call for both general ministry and the inevitable specific assignments. The initiative rests totally with Him. God simply chooses ordinary people with potential and abilities. The first disciples Jesus called were fishermen. They dropped their nets and followed him (Matt. 4:18-22). When Jesus called Simon Peter, he said, "You are Simon son of John. You will be called Cephas [Peter]" (John 1:42). Only Jesus can look at a person and say, "You are . . . but you will be!" Jesus saw what Simon could become when transformed by the Holy Spirit. Jesus saw what I could become too. He made me what I never thought I could be.

Jesus took responsibility for their success when He said, "Come with me. I'll *make* a new kind of fisherman out of you. I'll show you how to catch men and women instead of perch and bass" (Matt. 4:19, TM, emphasis added). There's no explanation as to why Jesus called common, ordinary fishermen except that He believed in them and gave them a vision larger than themselves. They were convinced that what they would be doing would have long-lasting significance. Jesus expanded their horizons by enlarging their expectations. Surely they felt drawn by an invisible power and were obliged to be attentive to whatever Jesus taught them to do.

Just as Christ called ordinary fishermen and used ordinary words to call them, my experience with God's call has at times seemed less like fireworks and more like a simple message. I've never experienced a lightning-bolt call when God had a special assignment for me. Paul refers to himself as "an apostle on special assignment for Christ . . . under God our Savior's command" (1 Tim. 1:1, TM). Ordinarily, Paul speaks of his apostleship as "by the will of God" (2 Tim. 1:1). Through the years, I have claimed this as God's desire for me to serve Him with all my heart where I am. Sometimes my assignments didn't feel so special, particularly in the midst of the turmoil associated with moving a church from the ruts of past habits into the vitality of new life.

There have been times during my comeback endeavors when I wondered if I was out of God's will when I accepted a particular assignment. I would look back to my point of decision and think, *I didn't see stars or lightning. Was I off base when I accepted this church?* But then I remembered that in all my years of ministry, shooting stars and lightning never happened. They still haven't. Instead, I've prayerfully responded to a sequence of God-ordained events that led me to accept the tough assignments. While God never once struck me with lightning, He has given me a deep inner peace that my decision was in His perfect will and that I, like Paul, was under Christ's command for the task at hand.

My decision-making process often took on the nuance of grappling with the call. For instance, in my early years I prayed, talked with family and friends, and then made a decision to accept a charge based on what felt right. When we were considering accepting a call to our fourth comeback assignment in Illinois, we openly discussed moving as a family from a large metropolitan city to that relatively small town of 34,000. My wife struggled more than the rest of us, because leaving meant giving up her good job and friends. We were seated at the kitchen table after church one night talking about moving when Jennifer, our eight-year-old daughter, asked if I had made up my mind yet. I asked her if she was praying.

She said, "I pray, but it's like I'm talking to myself."

I replied, "Jesus speaks to us in our hearts and tells us there."

Then she blurted out a prayer: "Lord, you know I want to move, so put it in my heart. Amen." No sooner had she finished than she erupted, "Praise the Lord—it's in there!" She jumped to her feet and lunged toward Kaye. She grabbed her mother's head in both hands and said, "Lord, put it in Mom's head too!"

I don't think that's exactly the kind of confirming proof Kaye needed, but eventually she acquiesced to my insistence that moving was God's will. Frankly, I had misgivings from the moment I accepted this comeback assignment but not enough to change my decision.

The Friday before I ended that seven-year pastorate, I received a phone call from one of our denominational leaders. "David," he said, "I think I may have the solution to your dilemma."

Stunned that he seemed to know my innermost thoughts, I responded, "And what dilemma is that?"

"I understand you may be unsettled about your decision to accept the church in Illinois," he replied. He had talked to mutual friends who knew of my misgivings. He proceeded to tell me about another church in need of a pastor if I had any interest.

"Why don't you and your wife fly out here tomorrow morning?" he suggested. "You can meet the church board at a luncheon in the airport hotel. Fly home, and let them vote on Sunday." Without so much as a pause for a response, he continued, "If the vote is favorable, you can simply tell the church in Illinois you've changed your mind and move here instead."

When I finally got a chance to speak, I said, "Hold on a minute. You're moving a little too fast. I'll have to think about this and pray too." Then I said, "Let me talk to my wife about it. She's still at work."

The last thing he said was, "The only thing worse than changing your mind is going to a place you really don't want to be."

As soon as I hung up the phone, I knew I had to decline this option. And I really didn't have to pray much about it. Common sense told me that even God doesn't change His mind that fast. I had made a decision that I believed I should honor. Nonetheless, Satan used those misgivings and the seed of doubt that had been planted about being "in a place you really don't want to be" to make me miserable for the first nine months in my new assignment. However, the Holy Spirit, in His mercy and patience, used scripture to bring me into full alignment with His will.

None of us is free of misgivings every second of every day in every assignment. Even in the midst of some of my assignments that I believed were God's will, I still experienced moments of doubt. If you've taken a comeback church and are wondering if you were crazy for even thinking about moving, be comforted. I've been there! I have grappled with a decision to move, then moved, then doubted the wisdom of my choice. However, God was always faithful to pull me through the mires of doubt and to honor my choice to emulate Paul as an apostle on "special assignment" for the Lord.

> *He bro't me out of the miry clay;*
> *He set my feet on the Rock to stay.*
> *He puts a song in my soul today—*
> *A song of praise, hallelujah!*
> —Henry L. Gilmour

Confirming Proof of a Promise

The tougher the assignment, the greater the need for confirming proof of God's will. Intellectually, you may use the rationale that God has successfully used you in previous comeback efforts. When I wrestled with acceptance of my most challenging comeback task, I was happily engaged in the successful comeback effort at Lakeview Church. I questioned my own sanity in leaving the comfort and security of a growing church to enter the war zone at another church. Was I ready for the arena of spiritual warfare? Apparently God thought so, but He had to convince me. I sought confirming proof from Scripture.

One day the reading was 1 Sam. 16. I read how Samuel protested being sent "to Jesse of Bethlehem" to choose Saul's successor from among his sons (v. 1). As I pondered accepting the call to the new church, I asked God the same thing Samuel did: "How can I go?" (v. 2). When the Lord clarified His plan for Samuel, saying, "I will show you what to do. . . . You are to anoint for me the one I indicate" (v. 3), Samuel didn't argue; he "did what the Lord said" (v. 4). I identified with Samuel's struggle to do the difficult thing God had asked him to do. As I read on, I empathized even further as Jesse's sons passed by Samuel one by one. Still, there was no sign from the Lord that God's chosen one had appeared.

"Are these all the sons you have?" Samuel inquired.

"There is still the youngest . . . but he is tending sheep," Jesse responded (v. 11).

Finally, David came before the prophet, and the Lord said, "Rise and anoint him; he is the one." Those words "he is the one" leaped from the page and into my heart as a burning call from God (v. 12). In a quiet and powerful way, the Word of God became my "lightning bolt."

Then Samuel anointed David "in the presence of his brothers, and from that day on the Spirit of the Lord came upon David in power" (v. 13). I fully expected the Lord's anointing to jump all over me as I said *yes*. What I received was quiet, confirming proof that this was God's will for me. No stars fell from the sky, but God's spirit invaded my room and specifically confirmed His calling.

Later, on the Saturday before my first day at the new church, the telephone rang at the parsonage. On the line was Wayne Farmer, my

Sunday School teacher when I was a teenager in Miami, who lived in the area but did not attend the church I would be pastoring. He had heard of my coming to this troubled church. After exchanging brief cordialities, he cut straight to the purpose of his call. "God has given me a promise to share with you as you begin tomorrow," he said with compassion in his voice. "The verse is Ps. 18:32—'It is God who arms me with strength and makes my way perfect.'" Goose bumps rose on my arms as I received confirming proof I was right where God wanted me to be. I noted the date in the flyleaf of my Bible and referred to that promise many times when the going got tough.

As with the Illinois assignment, this challenge presented difficult days filled with uncertainties and turmoil when I wondered if I had made the wrong choice. However, in my heart God always brought me back to that quiet, potent moment when He confirmed my call. And in my mind, He led me to the flyleaf of my Bible—to that concrete representation of an undeniably holy assignment. Remember—as you attempt to make your decision to accept the comeback church, bathe your heart in scripture, and then seal your promise with a written note of affirmation. These landmarks of certainty will sustain you during the difficult days that follow.

Joshua's Call

When God called Joshua to be Moses' successor, the assignment was to lead the Israelites across the Jordan River. Perhaps Joshua had observed what God could do with his reluctant predecessor. He may have wondered if he had the gifting to fulfill such a task. So God delivered a fresh promise of success if Joshua would "be strong and very courageous" (Josh. 1:7) and accept the responsibility. Sure enough, God gave him success in his very first leadership challenge: crossing the Jordan at floodtide. The comeback pastor holds much in common with Joshua. At times, God expects us to steer a church through floodwaters at what appears to be the most inopportune moment for change. However, Joshua's abandoned obedience opened the floodgates for a divine miracle. That miracle allowed an obedient leader and people to enter the Promised Land. Once there, however, before the conquest ever began, Joshua received what any of us on special assignment must have: a face-to-face encounter with God.

In Josh. 5, before Joshua led Israel in its first battle at Jericho, a man stood "in front of him with a drawn sword in his hand." He identified himself "as commander of the army of the LORD." Hearing those words, Joshua "fell facedown to the ground in reverence." When asked, "What message does my Lord have for his servant?" the Lord said, "Take off your sandals, for the place you are standing is holy. And Joshua did so" (vv. 13-15).

Joshua's Survival Discoveries

Joshua made four discoveries before his very first battle that sustained him throughout his tenure of conquest. These discoveries enabled me not only to survive but also to thrive in some fairly difficult assignments.

First, Joshua discovered that he wasn't alone. God told him, "As I was with Moses, so I will be with you; I will never leave you nor forsake you" (Josh. 1:5). Emotions and faith can become so jostled and jumbled that you can hardly find strength to face the daily struggles of normal living, let alone the major crises of leading a comeback effort. Psychologist Richard Blackmow said in a *Los Angeles Times* article that 75 percent of religious leaders go through a period of stress so great that they consider quitting.[3] When you're faced with difficult situations, the knowledge that you're not alone will sustain you and keep you from quitting.

So let me remind you that you're not alone. Is the pressure on? Are you bone tired? Have the stress and strain of the comeback struggle left you deflated and exhausted? Rendezvous with God. Lay this book aside. Get alone with Him, read His Word, and ask Him to speak to you as clearly as He spoke to Joshua. Let that fresh assurance bolster your sagging faith.

Pray out loud, *God, I know You brought me here. It's by Your will that I'm in this difficult place. I will rest in the knowledge that You are with me.* Reinforce your faith with these affirmations: *I will maintain faith no matter how tough things become, for I am Your child. You own me. I am Your property. I am Your responsibility. I may not understand how or why You have al-*

lowed me to pass through these things, but I am assured of Your infinite love and abiding presence. Give to me the courage You gave to Joshua. You are the same God. And I, like Joshua, am Your servant. Endow me with the power You bestowed upon him.

Second, Joshua discovered that the place where God put him was holy ground. This knowledge should enable you to endure when the work isn't running smoothly and things aren't going as planned. This is most difficult when the heartache and hurt are so real you believe those who brazenly say, "The church is doomed under your leadership." When doubts accost you and you fear that your best is not good enough, His presence makes your assignment holy ground.

Of course, laypeople face heartaches and hurts themselves. Their burdens are just as heavy. Everyone struggles at times with feelings of failure and frustration, and this sometimes leads to the conclusion that no one cares. Your Commander-in-Chief cares. His presence can make you adequate for every ministry challenge He gives you. Hear Him say, "The place where you're standing is holy."

Now affirm aloud as you read, *You will keep me here in Your love and give me grace in this trial to behave as Your child.* Now look up to the God of all grace and say to Him, *Your grace is sufficient for me. Forgive my whining and complaining. Enable me to behave as Your servant in a way that demonstrates faith.*

Third, Joshua discovered that God was in charge. Joshua was only a servant. How soon we forget that God is in command! There's great power in humbling ourselves before God and acknowledging that He's in control. If you can settle this important control issue before you find yourself on the battlefield, you'll be better prepared for future battles. Paul said, "So here's what I want you to do, God helping you: Take your everyday, ordinary life—your sleeping, eating, going-to-work, and walking-around life—and place it before God as an offering" (Rom. 12:1, TM). God wants control of your life and ministry. So bring the best you have to offer—you—and voluntarily say to God, *I give myself to You. Be in charge of any issue that comes up. You're the Boss.* Doing this will lead you to the highest, most fulfilling, balanced, happy life possible. To the contrary, if you choose to be in control—to call the shots every time—God will patiently wait until you're ready to let Him take over. The act of humbling yourself by giving control to Him is "holy and pleasing to God—this is your spiritual act of worship" (12:2).

Humbly bow before the Commander, and continue your prayer: *Make this time of testing a blessing, teaching me the lessons You intend for me to learn, and working in me the grace You intend to give. I choose to allow You to be in control. I know that my life is Father-filtered. I know that whenever I face trials of many kinds, the testing of my faith develops perseverance. "Perseverance must finish its work so that [I] may be mature and complete, not lacking anything"* (James 1:4).

Fourth, Joshua discovered that God had already won the battle. God gave Joshua a battle plan that involved marching around the walls once a day for six days. On the seventh day Joshua led the people around seven times, and on the seventh trip around, when the priests sounded the trumpet blast, they were to give a shout. Joshua followed the instructions with precision. The wall collapsed, and they took the city. To be successful in fighting the battles God has placed you in, you must allow Him to dictate the battle plan.

Perhaps today you need God to change your perspective. Here's a final faith affirmation: *I know the battle is Yours, Lord, not mine.* Although you're exhausted and anxious, finish this prayer: *I'm Yours. I'm on the winning side. I know You work on Your own schedule, not on one I might try to impose on You. I'll try to patiently wait, for in Your good time I know You'll bring me out again; how and when only You know.*

God's call sustained me in the difficult days that followed my acceptance of my sixth comeback church challenge. My confidence is that He'll do the same for any willing servant who abandons comfort for the sake of following God's call—even when that means entering an unholy war zone.

4 No-fault Decline

No service in itself is small,
None great, though earth it fill.
But that is small that seeks its own,
And great that does God's will.
—Anonymous

Let's not allow ourselves to get fatigued doing good. At the right time
we will harvest a good crop if we don't give up, or quit.
—Gal. 6:9, TM

In my fourth comeback church effort, a yearlong strike against a heavy-equipment manufacturer had ended about a month before we arrived. The 1983 recession had forced drastic cutbacks in the workforce at this company, where many of our people worked. The younger ones with low seniority were the first to be laid off as the workforce shrunk from a high of 38,000 to a low of 18,000. There were so many people leaving the community that bumper stickers began appearing on vehicles, urging, "Last one out, turn out the lights." Many tried to hang on in hopes of a callback until their last unemployment check was cashed. Many breadwinners in our church joined the ranks of the long-term unemployed. At first only a few families trickled away, always leaving the church on friendly terms. They loved their pastor, their church, and our town. We said goodbye at farewell fellowships, serving refreshments, presenting gifts along with hugs, handshakes, and tears. These emotional monthly meetings became so heartbreaking that we finally abandoned them. Over our four-year tenure, 200 church members moved away. For the first nine months, it was hard to encourage my people, because I was so discouraged myself.

Mistake or Mission?

I thought I had made the biggest mistake of my career. If God had not intervened on January 14, 1984, I may have resigned. In my devotions I read Heb. 3, the sad saga of Israel's unbelief and rebellion. When they faced their first crisis on the journey to Canaan (Exod. 17:1-7), they blamed Moses, complaining, "We never should have left Egypt." In my situation they might have said, "We never should have left St. Louis!" Suddenly the words "Today, if you hear His voice, do not harden your hearts as you did in the rebellion" (Heb. 3:7) leaped off the page. Because God's people would not give up their resistance, God declared, "They shall never enter my rest" (3:11). The Holy Spirit had my full attention.

The 12th verse socked me between the eyes as I adapted it to myself: "See to it, brothers, that [David Nixon does not have] a sinful, unbelieving heart that turns away from the living God." Yes, I was resisting the work God had called me to do in this difficult assignment. I saw myself standing at a crossroads. I could either choose hardening of the heart and its accompanying unrest, or I could submit to God's will for me in this assignment. I wrote in the flyleaf of my Bible, "The light is beginning to dawn." That cold January morning I repented of my extended resistance, and almost instantly I entered God's rest. The Sabbath-rest remained for me (4:9).

You may be in a place you really don't want to be. Things aren't going well. The losses seem insurmountable. Take some advice from a seasoned veteran: If God sent you there, don't resist Him, but let Him lead you to His rest.

I needed to relax in the sufficiency of God's power. When I released my anxiety to God, I received His peace in return. Relax in Him. Stop your worrying and fretting. Resistance only depletes your energy. Obedience will replenish your sagging spirit. From that moment on, when I said *yes* to God's assignment, I settled in to four productive years of ministry in a community wracked by economic recession.

Your Attitude Is Everything

Almost immediately my attitude began to change. The attitude you take when you find yourself leading a comeback in circumstances beyond your control determines whether you "soar on wings as eagles" or sag in the mire of your difficulties. The exodus affected the church financially, and there never seemed to be a loss of needy people to serve. People, not pocketbooks, had to remain our priority.

To lessen the demoralizing impact of our losses, I suggested we change our attitude toward them. Since we did not have the luxury of choosing our circumstances, our only choice was the attitude we would take toward them. "Faced with a continual outflow of people," I reasoned, "why not consider ourselves a sending church?" That's what the church in Antioch (Acts 13:3) became as they laid hands on Paul and Barnabas and sent them to the work God had ordained them to do. If outside circumstances cause members to leave your congregation, why not encourage the people to consider another way of thinking about the losses? I pleaded with church members to send people out to serve rather than to whine about our devastating losses. The attitude of the church changed dramatically.

Did I ever lapse into discouragement? Of course. I can't overstate how disheartening it is to watch a steady stream of people leave your church for reasons beyond your control. If my sense of success had been tied to the number of people I retained, I would have stayed in the pits. A sense of gloom permeated the church for about as long as I wrestled with the Lord about why He put me in a place like this! When my attitude changed, so did the attitudes of the people. Incidentally, at the end of four years, a new bumper sticker had appeared in the community: "Keep the lights on. I'm staying." Attitude is everything.

"Ghost Town Disease"

A church in eastern Texas struggles to average 20 in attendance. Over the nine years the bivocational pastor has led the church, the makeup of his congregation has changed. He has conducted numerous funerals during his tenure. When I sat down with the church to talk about the vision for the future, I received a realistic assessment of the situation. There are about 70 churches in the county—20 in this town of fewer than 3,000. Every major denomination is represented. The largest church runs fewer than 300. Not everyone is leaving town, but there's nothing to keep the young people there. When they graduate from high school, most move on to other places where there's more opportunity. With few if any new people moving into this old town, the population is rapidly aging. The employment opportunities are limited to teaching in the county school system, working in the local paper factory, or opening an antique shop, bed and breakfast, or restaurant in the historic district.

What C. Peter Wagner calls "ghost town disease"[1] is happening to this historic town. This sociological factor is beyond the control of the pastor and the people. Their small church board is realistic about its inability to network with the dwindling pool of unchurched residents. It's understood that younger couples will likely go to the larger churches because of the programs or ministries already in place. I asked whether this church would be here in 10 years and was shocked to hear a resounding *yes*.

I urged the board members to look for ministry or mission opportunities in their community. The more we talked, the more excited they became as they began to identify opportunities on the horizon to reach people for Christ. They have begun a prayer ministry to people in the community. They work their way through the phone book alphabetically and simply ask dial-ups for prayer requests the church can pray about. They also plan to canvass their community with three-by-five cards asking for prayer requests. Even small churches need to keep looking for new outreach opportunities. As Wagner suggests, "The secret of success for churches [in declining areas] is to find a need and fill it, or find a hurt and heal it."[2]

Survival Strategies in a Declining Community

Never discount the work of God that takes place in small churches in declining areas. Our efforts in our first comeback were rewarded with some big victories and some significant progress. When we arrived at the Spacecoast community on the east coast of Florida, the church secretary described my first church as "looking up to see bottom." Changes in the community had contributed to the decline of the church. We arrived there in the early 1970s, when the Apollo space program was experiencing drastic cutbacks. Scientists and support technicians who had tied their futures to the soaring Apollo rockets were laid off when the program was grounded. The shells of unfinished luxury homes lined the streets of many neighborhoods. The church wasn't responsible for this "local contextual factor."

As a matter of fact, our church more than doubled in attendance. But more important, lives were changed. One man whose marriage had crumbled when his wife ran off with another man came to Christ. In the two short years we ministered at this church, he became grounded in his walk with God. God called him to preach, he remarried, and he's now serving effectively as a minister of the gospel.

The success of God's work is not measured by the size of your church but by your faithfulness to your calling and the holy things that happen in your church—big and small. In a small church that has to look up to see the bottom, you may have to serve as custodian, lawn care specialist, preacher, teacher, youth pastor, and a whole lot more. The choir director may lead a faithful few singers with a two-year-old in one arm as she directs with the other. The same singers may sing all the specials. You may have to hold down a full-time job because the church can't afford to pay a full-time salary.

If God doesn't despise the day of small things (Zech. 4:10), should we? Bigger is not better in God's eyes. God uses small things, small churches, and even small-minded people to accomplish big purposes. Here are some strategies that will work in a comeback church experience in the throes of a declining community.

1. Accentuate the positive; eliminate the negative.

When you're looking up to see bottom, you must resist negativism with all your might. More than once my preacher dad told me, "Accentuate the positive and eliminate the negative." Don't feed your people a steady diet of negativism—particularly if you find yourself in a discouraging financial situation. Negativism is always counterproductive. I recall giving the people a steady menu of "Think About It" bulletin clips designed to identify the kind of people I thought were sitting in the pews. The bulletin questions always fell under the heading "Which of these are you?" Here are some examples:

- Some members keep their organization strong,

While others join just to belong.
- Some volunteer and do their share,
  While some lie back and just don't care.
- On meeting days, some always show,
  While there are those who never go.
- Some always pay their dues ahead;
  Some get behind for months instead.
- Some lag behind—some let things go
  And never help their group to grow.
- Some drag, some pull;
  Some don't, some do.

This ill-advised idea was to shame the people to a deeper level of commitment and involvement. Such a negative approach did little to change behavior and should be avoided at all cost.

2. Model caring concern.

In a church looking up to see bottom, you may have to model caring concern long before the people ever pitch in to help you. Disheartened people must be taught to care about the appearance of the buildings and grounds. The previously mentioned pastor in the near ghost town has taken the initiative in several beautification projects at his 1940s wood frame building. His people have responded to the caring concern he has demonstrated. The buildings have received a facelift with fresh paint. There's now a nursery for the babies. Most recently, a new steeple was installed. Your church may be in a declining community, but you must take the lead in saying, "We care." You must model caring concern.

3. Assume a servant's role.

If you're the pastor in a declining community, you may be called to be a worker, shepherd, and caretaker. The first church I served was in a very visible location across the street from a university campus. The church building occupied three acres of sparse grass and sand. Growing up in a parsonage, I learned the importance of keeping God's house clean and attractive. This meant a tidy interior and a neatly trimmed exterior.

Who takes responsibility to see that this happens in a small church that can't afford to pay someone to do it? The answer is the one who cares the most. I wanted the property to look neat for Sundays, so a major portion of Fridays and Saturdays was spent mowing the lawn. The church's riding mower didn't work, so we switched to our own push mower! Occasionally a helpful teen showed up to assist, but largely the mowing responsibility fell to us.

One day near the end of the week I was away for a district meeting. My wife knew that I wouldn't make it back in time to mow, so she set out to mow an acre of grass with our 21-inch push mower. There was no one to watch our toddler, so Kaye pushed the mower with one hand and pulled Sonya along with the other. A local newspaper reporter happened by and spotted a photo opportunity. Guess whose picture made the front page the next day? Even that publicity didn't bring forth any additional help for the time being. Fortunately, though, we began to get help with the work as time went on.

Uncut grass, weather-beaten trim, and peeling paint say to the community, "We *don't* care." God had called me to preach, but in a small church looking up to see bottom, that may mean also joyfully serving as caretaker of the building and grounds.

4. Start new ministries even if you have to lead them yourself.

In the 1970s many of us caught Jack Hyles's vision for bus ministry. Scores of children and young people—some dragging their parents behind—poured into the church from a decrepit but freshly painted church bus. In our first comeback effort, as soon as the money was provided and a bus could be located, my wife and I set out knocking on doors in the community looking for boys and girls to ride the bus to Sunday School. Within a few short weeks, more than 20 riders were breathing new life into our Sunday School and church. A small corps of children's church workers were trained and mobilized under my wife's leadership to teach in our rapidly growing children's department. Within eight weeks, we had firmly established our bus route, giving us a steady flow of new prospects into the church.

In 1983, my fourth comeback church still had four bus routes in operation staffed by a corps of faithful workers, many of whom had been won to Christ through the bus ministry. On any given week we could put on a push and bring in more than 100 children and teens, so attendance figures remained fairly consistent in the face of our losses. To this day, that church still operates a bus ministry. Many churches have long since abandoned the idea of looking for boys and girls who need the Lord. Some churches believe they have moved beyond this unsophisticated method of reaching people and have decided that they're getting no bang for their bucks by bringing in boys and girls who could not begin to pay for what the outreach costs.

Bus ministry is hard work. I know. I worked to establish bus routes in at least two churches that didn't have them. I know I wasn't as diligent in reaching the moms and dads of our bus riders as I should have been. We inflated our numbers but eventually came to the conclusion that mostly we were providing free babysitting for unsaved parents on Sunday mornings. When enough people complained and insurance issues were raised . . . when bus workers became difficult to recruit . . . when receipts in the offering plates did not match the outlay of expense, we quit. For many churches, bus ministry became an outdated method of a bygone era. Nothing since has come along to attract people for Christ as did the bus ministry. Only eternity will reveal the number of children who were won to Christ in the decade of the 70s and 80s, when churches of every size and description rolled their rickety buses through neighborhoods and into the hearts and lives of people.

Perhaps it's time to resurrect the bus ministry. If it's not conducive to your church, what is? Dare to start a new ministry!

A strong emphasis on youth ministry also contributed to the Spacecoast's comeback. My wife and I led the way in ministry to young people with the help of some dedicated volunteers. Weekly activities, retreats, and outings on the water enabled us to pull together a strong teen group. A choir was organized, and it ministered in the church in a monthly youth service and even toured other churches, presenting music and drama. The young people brought their friends from school, and the result was new life pumped into a declining church. The teens led the way in helping clean and paint the church. Gradually, more and more adults joined in. The foundation for an ongoing comeback was laid by starting new ministries and modeling and mentoring laypeople, then turning them loose to lead.

5. Accept "maintenance ministry" as viable.

The goal of ministry in a church suffering major losses through no fault of its own is to provide stability. Some would characterize this as a "maintenance" ministry. Even though many new people were won to Christ during those recession years, the church seemed to lose one member for every one it gained. This kept the statistics flat. The church had to grow just to maintain. For every two steps forward, we took one step backward. Not all ministers are content with a ministry of maintenance. If you have what Warren W. Wiersbe calls "the stepping-stone attitude of the pyramid climbers," maintenance ministry will not "do anything for you,"[3] and you'll leave as soon as something you think is better comes along.

Before you write that letter of resignation, consider that God has put you right where he wants you to teach you things you may learn no other way. And my hunch is that you've been far more successful than you think.

6. Minister to the real needs of people.

You'll find needy persons on almost any street, particularly those regions immersed in recession and high unemployment. In my third turnaround effort, the Care and Share ministry of local benevolence came into being to meet some of the irrepressible needs of the people. Over the first three years that an organized ministry of mercy to the needy was established, we ministered to more than 75 families, providing more than $6,500 in emergency relief.

At Christmas we sent checks to our unemployed or poor members. A fellow pastor with a family of seven earning less than $4,000 per year received cash, food, and gifts. When fire destroyed the house one of our families, the church was there to provide support. A family in the community facing eviction asked for help, and we were able to give it.

A young mother of four small children, abandoned by her husband and trying to survive on Aid to Dependent Children, discovered that the electricity could not be turned on in her apartment until her husband's delinquent bill—incurred before they were married—was paid. When we learned that she had no electricity and no means of cooking other than on a charcoal grill and no means of hot baths and so on, the bad debt was paid so that power could be restored.

When fire destroyed a family's sole means of transportation and there was no insurance to replace it, money was donated toward the purchase of a replacement vehicle so that the husband could continue to provide for his family.

The wells of government assistance were drying up, and the church could not depend upon the government to do its benevolence work. A caring response to the poor and needy was developed.

When a family in the church faced the loss of their home because their taxes were delinquent, one of my greatest joys in ministry occurred the day I delivered a check to the office of the county clerk redeeming the member's home. The county clerk issued a certificate of redemption when the delinquent real estate taxes, penalties, and costs were paid in full.

Caring, compassionate church members saved a fellow member's home. About a year before, the members of this same family had knelt at the altar of the church and accepted Christ as Savior and Lord. This dear family was twice redeemed—saved by a loving Savior who redeemed them for heaven, saved by a compassionate church who redeemed their home.

7. Leave the results to God.

People in declining communities need the caregiving ministry of the church. Rather than becoming discouraged and frustrated by conditions over which you have no control, take your marching orders from God's Word, and leave the results to God. In *Wake Up! You Have a Ministry* Dave Ray suggests,

> Perhaps we need to redefine what being God's servant really is. In human terms a servant asks the master what needs to be done and then proceeds to do it. The human servant is responsible to listen to his master's commands and for the results. God's servant is responsible to be faithful to God's commands, but the results are God's. God wants to work through us, and we will succeed if we let Him.[4]

You Can't Just Sit There

At this phase of my ministry, I'm responsible for overseeing 70 churches, and I'm required to address each of these churches about once a year. During one of my sermons, I often focus on Luke 5:17-26. In this passage is a group of people described by Luke as just "sitting there" (5:17). These Pharisees and teachers of the law always seemed to clash with Jesus over some point of law. On this particular day these professional religionists—avid churchgoers—were on hand to see a good show. Like so many who sit in our pews, they were apathetic as they skeptically waited to witness a miracle. They weren't the least bit concerned that their presence might prevent someone from receiving a miracle. The room was crowded, and, more important, "the power of the Lord was present" (v. 17). This lent some urgency to what was about to unfold. The stretcher-bearers seized their window of opportunity. No way were they going to just sit there with a needy friend when a healing Savior was within reach!

The four men carrying the paraplegic on a stretcher could not get in because of the crowded conditions. Quickly they sized up the situation and showed remarkable determination. Bent on getting their friend into the presence of Jesus, they carried the stretcher up a flight of stairs to the roof. Not one of them by himself could have carried the paraplegic. But together, each man carried his corner of the stretcher. Each doing his part, they lowered the man into the presence of Jesus.

You cannot do everything, but you *can* do *something*. Even if there are obstacles to overcome, you must first believe that you can do something. And then, like these stretcher-bearers, you can enlist people who will work with you to bring hurting people to Jesus. Unfortunately, if your people have been just sitting there unmotivated for ages, your first challenge will be to get them off their seats and onto their feet and to hit the streets to do something significant for God. Somebody served as captain of that four-man team who lowered the stretcher. That's your assignment as a comeback pastor in a small church.

Motivational Fuels for the Pew Sitter

- **Show them how to love.** In the words of the popular song, many churches have "lost that lovin' feelin'." A lack of love prevents the church from reaching those who do not know Christ. Rekindle love, and your church will become attractive to outsiders. Become a church that cares, and you'll begin to draw unchurched people.

- **Focus attention on serving others.** The tendency in a small church is to become so self-focused that all we see are the faults and shortcomings of the saints. Begin to care, share, give, and serve. Kennon L. Callahan tells of a church that had been dying for years. One of the elderly members who attended one of his seminars said, "We were down to 14 people, in our 70s and 80s. We knew it wouldn't be long before our church was dead, done, and gone." But they began to focus on serving rather than surviving. That handful of senior citizens got busy in their community serving in their local school, and their compassion was contagious—and attractive. Callahan asserts, "High-compassion, high-community congregations will thrive in coming years."[5]

- **Win a new person to Christ.** Nothing rekindles the fire of enthusiasm in a church like seeing a new believer transformed by the grace of God. Many small churches go year after year without winning a single new person to Christ. You're faced with a choice. Will you bemoan the fact that you have no one gifted in evangelism? Or will you fast, pray, believe, and work until God gives you one new convert? Start with one, and then go after another. See what God will do.

- **Awaken the sleeping giant.** The Bible is clear (Eph. 4:12) that every believer has a ministry that's a gift from God himself. He or she doesn't have to do what others may be gifted to do, but everyone can minister in the areas of his or her skills, talents, and experiences. God needs everyone. No service is too small or too insignificant for God to use. Each person has a part in the harvest. When your people see that each seemingly unimportant effort contributes to the task of winning others to Christ, they'll throw themselves wholeheartedly into serving the Lord—yes, even in areas where the demographics scream, "Decline!" People still need the Lord.

5 The Forced-out Pastor

Many a pastor has hobbled away from his serving and could not rekindle the passionate fire of God's calling again for just such a cause.
—John Schmidt

Give a bonus to leaders who do a good job, especially the ones who work hard at preaching and teaching.
—1 Tim. 5:17, TM

The Associated Press in 1996 posted some interesting findings about the clergy. David Goetz of *Leadership* was quoted as saying, "Today may be the worst time to lead a church."[1] A questionnaire mailed to a selected group of 1,000 pastors indicated the following responses:

- Nearly 25 percent of pastors said they had been fired or forced to resign.
- A third said that at their present church assignment, their predecessor had been forced out.
- Approximately 43 percent said that a "faction" had pushed them, and 71 percent of those said the faction was fewer than ten people.
- Six out of ten of the forced-out pastors said the experience negatively affected their family's ability to trust the established church. Two-thirds said the experience positively affected their faith and their prayer life.
- About 53 percent of the forced-out pastors blamed themselves for not asking adequate questions of the church before accepting the call.
- Around 80 percent of practicing pastors believe ministry negatively affects them and/or their families.

Bob Mowrey, completing a record tenure of 35 years at his church, told the *Nashville Banner* religion editor, "Vast changes in society and in the makeup of congregations are causing some ministers 'to get their hearts torn out today.'"[2] The article noted that 2,000 pastors of a prominent Evangelical denomination had been asked to leave their churches since 1994.

Why are so many ministers facing forced termination today? H. B. London and Neil B. Wiseman in *Pastors at Risk* offer the assessment that pastoring is harder now than ever before: "Many pressing contemporary difficulties were largely unknown in earlier periods of Christian history. Change seems to be in the driver's seat in today's culture and the church."[3]

Pastors live on the raw edge of life and find themselves in a constant whirlwind of stressful events. Many of the forced-out pastors cited above felt that the church they served expected the pastor to produce an increase in finances and membership without changing the comfortable routines of the older members. Pastors are expected to wear several administrative hats, increase attendance and finances, oversee building repairs, recruit staff and volunteers, and on top of all this prepare stimulating multiple sermons, messages, and Bible lessons each week. If a pastor fails in any given area, he or she may face force-out.

No wonder "pastoral AWOL is on the increase," as London and Wiseman note. "The problem is so large that church leaders fear not enough battle-ready soldiers will be available to impact the remainder of this decade or the new century. No one can guess what the defection rate will be when the fight becomes more fierce, as it will. And the battle fatigue of those who remain will thwart their productivity."[4]

John Schmidt of Garden Ministries describes this alarming and dangerous trend: "Many a pastor hobbled away from his serving and could not rekindle the passionate fire of God's calling again for just such a cause. The flame was snuffed out by the mocking 'ahas' and condemning smirks of Satan's hordes who gleefully turn their attention to the next in line to be devoured."[5] While we cannot control the downgrading of pastors in our society, should we not seek to control the same by those within the church? The curse of forced termination is ripping the hearts out of godly men and women in nearly every denomination. "The future of ministry is in crisis because fewer exemplary candidates are answering God's call to ministry," conclude London and Wiseman.[6]

An Epidemic of Forced Termination

The reality is that many are leaving the ministry in droves because a bad situation has made continuance impossible. Varying surveys put the annual number of smitten shepherds stepping out somewhere between 17,000 and 50,000. I had no idea such a massive amount of pastors were leaving the ministry each year. These numbers are astonishing and, according to John Schmidt, "could be one of the biggest church events in North America,"[7] especially when most of these people stepped aside through some form of forced termination. What is unknown is whether the firings came as a result of misfortune or mistakes. There is considerable bloodletting, and not all pastors have slit their own throats.

Forced termination is the term for the circumstance that removes the majority of the pastors from their work. Forced-out pastors may be removed from their work, but rarely are they separated from their calling. An excruciatingly painful toll is taken on both the pastor and his or her entire family. For a moment, try to put yourself in the place of the forced-out pastor. When the sad day of departure finally arrives, the grieving pastor finds himself or herself out of work with no visible means of support. Most of these wounded shepherds receive no severance pay. All too frequently they're left alone in their pain. Few have one close friend they can lean on at a time when they need support the most. Even their colleagues avoid them as if they have the plague, probably because they are ill prepared to know what to say or do. Unlike David in Adullam's cave (1 Sam. 22), they have no one who rushes to them to stand with them or to offer support.

I now work with church boards to call new pastors. At times I'm asked to assist a candidate who was forced out of a previous church. They might receive a brief glance but usually are not seriously considered. The assumption is made that if a pastor is forced out, it must be his or her fault. The fear is that what happened once could happen again. A forced-out pastor might as well wear a scarlet "T" on his or her back that stands for "Trouble," as far as search committees or church boards are concerned.

With so many forced terminations in North American churches, the likelihood is that you may be called to follow a forced-out pastor at some point in your career. My third comeback church experience was a church in the Midwest that had voted out its pastor. Consider the case of one of my predecessors, Harold Hickman (all names have been changed).

Close Is Not Good Enough

Rev. Hickman could have avoided being forced out had he mustered just a few more votes. The rule was that the pastor must receive a two-thirds favorable membership vote in order to stay. Harold received 66⅓ percent. It was announced that Bro. Hickman would remain as pastor.

But then Boyd Marley stood to his feet and asked to be recognized. "Mr. Chairman," he said, "excuse me, but you must have flunked math. According to my calculations, two-thirds favorable vote would need to be 66⅔ percent. Didn't you say the vote was 66⅓ percent?" The congregation sat in stunned silence as he continued, "I believe that Bro. Hickman missed it by a third of a percent."

As everyone waited, the superintendent quickly recalculated the tellers' math in much the same way a referee reviews a contested play in a football game. This was no game, however. A pin drop would have sounded like a clap of lightning. As seconds dragged into minutes, the embarrassed leader looked up in dismay and, choking back tears, announced, "After further review, the call is changed." As if to defend his error, he continued, "I wanted to give Bro. Hickman the benefit of the close call."

From his seat two-thirds of the way back on the speaker's right, Boyd Marley smirked with an I-gotcha-on-this-one smile. "I don't think that would be a legal vote, do you?"

Publicly embarrassed into compliance, the leader had to admit that Bro. Marley was correct. He then announced that Bro. Hickman would not continue as pastor after all. Thirty days later, Harold Hickman moved on. The devastating fallout from his being forced out began as those sympathetic to Harold and his wife began to pack up and leave. Harold made just two strategic mistakes of the self-inflicted kind in his start-up days that literally cost him his ministry at the Overton church.

The epidemic of force-outs is real, and some pastors like Bro. Hickman make mistakes from which they cannot recover before the voting members get a ballot in their hands. I've only scratched the surface on this issue, but my early conclusions are that force-outs come for reasons that can be the faults of either the pastor or laypeople. The three main reasons are blunders, betrayals, and bullying or abuse.

Blunders

Harold Hickman's blunders were centered on predecessor issues, as we'll see. His mistakes should be avoided whether you follow a long-term, beloved pastor or not.

1. Refusing to accept what's provided.

Harold Hickman accepted a call to pastor after a man with 34 years tenure. W. A. Allbright had planted the church and spent his life's ministry in that assignment. An entire generation had grown up under his ministry. He was deeply loved and highly esteemed. When Bro. Hickman arrived, W. A. Allbright remained an active member of the congregation as a retired elder. As difficult as that was, that was not his first mistake.

On the day of Rev. Hickman's arrival, the moving company deposited their belongings in the parsonage, but the minister and his wife would not unpack them. Instead, Harold hastily called a board meeting and reportedly said, "We're used to better than this. I'd like a housing allowance instead." The board acquiesced to his demands, leaving the parsonage vacant until a staff member moved in. The Hickmans failed to consider that the parsonage had been quite adequate for the Allbrights for the past 17 years. What Harold said really doesn't matter. What he communicated was that he considered their parsonage substandard and that he was selfish enough not to consider how the church members would feel about his complaints. Harold's first blunder was a serious bump in the road, but not a life-threatening episode.

2. Demanding rather than earning respect.

Harold's second blunder was his insistence that the people immediately transfer their love and loyalty to him. His actions revealed that he perceived the people's love for his predecessor as a personal affront. I can understand the temptation to view a predecessor in this vein. Conversely, I can understand that the people would naturally struggle to give loyalty to the new pastor. People begin to follow their pastor because he or she is their leader. If only Harold had patiently worked to gain their respect, perhaps they would have kept following him. Instead, his actions following the death of his predecessor showed that Harold really felt he deserved their respect. "Respect," writes John Maxwell, "is a matter of leadership—not position, title, or gender."[8]

A year into Hickman's tenure at the church, W. A. Allbright had a massive, fatal heart attack. The church mourned his passing for months. No one stopped loving W. A. Really, if Harold had understood that respect is earned over time, the people would have eventually loved him too. His impatience led to another critical blunder.

3. Refusing to give honor.

Soon after Bro. Allbright died, his family asked Pastor Hickman if they could hang a portrait in the hallway as a way of honoring him in the church to which he had given his entire ministry. Harold's response was quite unimaginable. "Well," he said, "if you hang a picture of him, you'll have to hang one of me as well." End of discussion. The family headed for the door, incredulous at what they had just heard. When word of the incident traveled through the grapevine, some lost respect for Bro. Hickman. The more mature members dismissed another blunder. Still others were so offended by Harold's self-serving behavior that when they got their chance, their anger erupted into a "no" vote.

Unless you are the first pastor (church planter) digging out a new work, you'll have a predecessor or will be one at some point in your career. To earn the respect of those you try to lead, you must follow these guidelines:

- **Respect yourself and those around you.** Respect begets respect. Treat people and those they love as you desire to be treated.
- **Do a little more than what's expected or required.** Bruce Wilkerson calls such a person a "gimper."[9] Gimpers for the Lord, who exceed the expectations of their people without calling attention to what they do, add huge deposits in the bank of respect.
- **Work at being credible, not clever.** You cannot take shortcuts and expect to be known for integrity. Truth always comes out. To paraphrase John Maxwell, "Ministry is like a vise; at times it will squeeze us. At those moments of pressure, whatever is inside will be found out. We cannot give what we do not have. Image promises much but produces little. Integrity never disappoints."[10] So strive to keep your integrity intact, and trust and respect will soon follow.

- **Become known as a problem solver, not a problem creator.** Most people have more than their share of unsolicited problems. A pastor who can soothe problems rather than stir them earns credibility and respect. When there's a problem, don't *be* one, and you just might quiet more rumbles than you cause.
- **Keep your attitude in check.** Nothing turns people off more quickly than a bad attitude. You can't control your circumstances, but you certainly are responsible for your attitude toward them. Your attitude will affect the attitudes of the people you're trying to lead. Let them catch a good attitude from you, and don't be surprised if another major deposit goes into your bank account of respect.

4. **Upsetting the power structure.**

Another of my predecessors, Brad, innocently blundered into an upset of the existing power structure of his church. Like it or not, every church has such an "unstated" structure. The power may reside in a committee, the church board, several key influencers, or in some cases only one strong person. The power in Brad's church seemed to reside in a longstanding executive committee who had exercised strong leadership for many years. These capable, highly motivated men—the movers and shakers—commanded respect. Their strong bias toward action expedited the decision-making process. The church had experienced steady growth into the 700s. After Brad arrived, some newer board members began to feel that their only role was to rubber-stamp decisions that had already been made by the executive committee. They wanted to share in the power. Brad sympathized with the newer members and decided that the board would share in the decision-making processes of their rapidly growing church.

Before Brad arrived, the predecessor had been quite comfortable with letting these capable businessmen run the business of the church. They freely sacrificed to see that the church had the money to carry out its mission. When the church broke ground for relocation to a highly visible part of town, interest rates were at eight percent. But by the time the construction loan could be finalized, interest rates had skyrocketed to 20%. The executive committee monitored the finances on a weekly basis. Whenever there was a shortfall, I'm told they took out their checkbooks to make up the difference. No wonder they felt a strong sense of ownership. They had bought and paid for their church. Many other faithful members followed their example, cashing in paid-up life insurance policies and giving the proceeds to the church. Such sacrifice paid rich dividends in growth and blessing. Scores of people came to Christ during the decade.

During his tenure, Brad's predecessor and the executive committee began to believe that a strong music program would give them a competitive edge, so they hired one of the best ministers of music in the denomination. In order to match Ken's package at a larger church, members of the executive committee personally made up the difference in financial incentives to get him to come to their church. They had literally bought and paid for Ken and his wife, Carla. Their energetic music program further enhanced the church's growth and ministry. The church's Easter productions were the talk of the entire city, but still, they had not broken the 1,000 barrier.

Then Brad's predecessor resigned. Once again the executive committee became the members of the search committee to find a new pastor. They searched and found one of the finest, young, up-and-coming pastors in the denomination—Brad. They believed that surely his charisma and preaching skills combined with a fantastic music program would take them to the next level. By any human calculation, that should have been the case. With great music, dynamic worship, and Brad's powerful preaching, momentum soared. The church began to break the 1,000 barrier in attendance on a consistent basis, though some later doubted the accuracy of the counts. Great crowds were common.

Then one day Pastor Brad made a simple but fatal mistake. He succumbed to pressure from his figurehead board to change the way decisions had been made at the church for at least 15 years. The executive committee was dismantled. The entire board would then make all major decisions. Now impotent rather than important, key members of the defunct executive committee resigned from the board. However, they continued their roles as the influencers on significant numbers of church members.

What is so wrong with a power structure? Who judges what group of people will lead? When does the power structure cross the line of corruptibility? I think the line is crossed when power vested becomes ownership, when "our" church becomes "my" church. In those early days as Brad's successor, the disenfranchised would remind me, "We built this church. We paid the bills when no one else could. We've been here all our lives." "My, me, mine," permeated every conversation. Brad made a big blunder, but that was not the sole reason for his forced termination.

Pastoral and Congregational Betrayals

In *Setting Your Church Free*, Neil Anderson is adamant: "No pastor will survive disloyalty."[11] Most large churches give the senior pastor the prerogative to hire his or her own staff. But an unwritten rule persists in many churches with long-term associates: "Don't mess with existing staff." Invariably, pressure is applied to the denominational leadership and potential candidates to "opt" to retain a favorite associate. Such an appeal is made using the argument of continuity. They might as well hang a sign on the pastor's office door: "Tamper with existing staff at your own peril."

The church board insisted that Brad Parker retain Ken. Details of what actually transpired next are sketchy at best. But Brad knew within the first 90 days that he and Ken had reached an impasse in their ability to work together. When word leaked out that Pastor Brad and Ken could not work together, key members of the now-defunct executive committee championed Ken's cause. After all, they reasoned, Ken had been there before Brad came, and as far as they were concerned, he would be there when Brad left. Just who perpetrated the taking of "sides" is difficult to call. Blame should probably be shared for forcing the people to choose between the two. Regardless, the congregation was forced to take either the pastor's or the associate's side. Those who loved and respected both men were caught in the middle. Many folks quit the church rather than choose a side.

By mutual consent Brad and Ken agreed to part company. Their "confidential" agreement went public minutes after the decision. Ken's supporters believed that he had been fired, and he did nothing to correct that perception. Accusations were lobbed back and forth like hand grenades. Some of the old executive committee members led a fierce campaign to pressure Brad to resign.

For a time before Ken left when Brad stood up to preach, his opponents in the balcony unfolded newspapers in protest and began to read. When that contemptuous tactic failed to deter Brad, Ken's sympathizers walked out in protest after he finished his ministry in the service. As more and more people witnessed the escalating debacle, attendance plummeted. To further pressure the church to give them what they wanted, many of Ken's backers withheld their tithe. It's believed that some of them then paid their tithe to Ken. Income drastically dropped.

Pastor Brad quickly replaced Ken, hoping that somehow he could weather the storm. But the sub-Christian behavior became destructive. Brad's opponents egged the parsonage. His wife and children received threatening phone calls. This untold damage was done in the name of Jesus Christ! The eternal consequences may never be known until the final judgment. Attendance plummeted from a high of 1,000 to below 600 before Brad saw no recourse but to resign.

Bullying or Abuse

In one growing church where Ron Snow pastored, five people lodged accusations against him at his regular pastoral review. The following day the district superintendent met with Ron to recount the concerns expressed by his board. Ron needed time to think about how to address the concerns. Christmas festivities were approaching, so Ron asked to postpone the meeting until after the holidays.

After the first of the year, the board administrative committee met with the denominational leader, Dr. Crook, to discuss issues and concerns about church unity. Two days later they asked that Ron meet jointly with a reconciliation counselor for guidance. He acquiesced to their request. Two weeks later, the administrative committee, Dr. Crook, and Ron met, and a plan of reconciliation was contrived to correct the alleged breach in relationship.

The reconciliation plan imposed actions on Ron's part intended to resolve the problem. First, he had to reconcile with the administrative committee and church board by confessing (agreeing with) their perceived grievances. Second, he had to seek forgiveness from individuals within the congregation from a list submitted by his board. Their idea was that by modeling reconciliation, Ron would then be able to lead the reconciliation process with individuals within the congregation who had grievances with each other.

Third, Ron had to commit to join an accountability support group and a prescribed accountability plan. Expectations were outlined that were to be monitored, encouraged, and supported by these accountability monitors. Ron's "God squad" would report to the church board each month over the next year.

After the board approved the plan of public humiliation, Dr. Crook met with Ron to emphasize the importance of his making a public confession in the Sunday morning service. In compliance, Ron dutifully read his leader's confession of "failure to communicate with the church board in a timely and effective manner." As contritely as he could fake, Ron asked forgiveness for things he did not believe he had done in an attempt to help the church be reconciled to God and each other.

Three days later, the administrative committee met with Dr. Crook to draft an expectation outline for Pastor Ron's behavioral modification. The five-point plan required the following:

1. **Receive exhortation and reprimand.** Since only two names were mentioned, Ron and his wife assumed they would do most of the confessing and that the "morality monitors" would do the exhorting and rebuking. Ron was expected to cower in confessional humiliation before whomever the board said he owed an apology—in their opinion.

2. **Build confidence and trust.** Ron was to set an example in honest self-disclosure in his conversations, to follow through on his commitments, and to give priority to fine-tuning an organizational system that would keep him on track with dates, appointments, plans, commitments, "and so forth."

3. **Lead as a "watchman of the night."** Ron must convey the vision/mission to the church body, facilitate resources in the church to carry out the mission, develop an overall strategy for equipping the body, develop staff, set goals, receive feedback, and plan worship services while actively seeking input and direction from committees, the board, and his denominational leader. And, by the way, Ron and his wife were

to take at least one day a week to be away from all the imposed ministry responsibilities.

4. Set an example in finances. Ron's financial responsibilities were to be delegated. Purchases over a set amount needed board approval. He would have input in major financial decisions and expenditures, but never without someone looking over his shoulder.

5. Discipline himself in all matters spiritual. Ron was forced to be accountable for his personal prayer and Bible study time as well as his leadership of staff in accordance with a board-approved plan of spiritual formation. In addition, his preaching, counseling, and finally, pastoral care would be closely monitored.

Ron was to report on each of the above, indicating how much time he actually spent carrying out each aspect of their suffocating list of expectations. The "God squad" crossed the line, in my opinion, when they imposed some highly invasive "accountability questions":

a. Are you spending time alone with God?

b. Is your thought life pure?

c. What are your motives?

d. Are you walking in obedience to God?

e. Have you lied in answering any of the previous questions?

After reviewing their lengthy list of expectations with Ron, the committee made a move designed to bring his wife in line with their expectations of a pastor's spouse. The alleged purpose was to increase understanding and continue the reconciliation process. Ron acquiesced to the bullying of the accountability plan, but when they tried to put his wife in the same straightjacket, Ron said no. A few days later, Ron submitted his resignation to Dr. Crook.

Ron was forced out by a small but influential group of people who bullied their pastor in an effort to put him in his place. In three short months, another godly warrior departed from the battle arena, a victim of betrayal or bullying or both.

As heart-wrenching as the above scenario is, the fact remains that sometimes pastors aren't the victims of bullying or abuse. They're the perpetrators. Take, for instance, the example of the unscrupulous pastor one of my predecessors followed.

During his first week at that Midwest church, Duane received a phone call from an official summoning him to the local bank. There he was informed that $140,000 in unsecured demand notes signed by his predecessor in the church's name had come due. The congregation was obligated for debt it had not voted to incur. When I arrived at this church, I discovered that a man named Leonard had loaned this unethical pastor $25,000 to buy a new luxury car on a verbal promise that the money would be repaid. Leonard never heard from him again. You can imagine his hurt and anger at having been cheated out of a big chunk of his retirement savings. Leonard asked me to help him get his money back. That pastor surrendered his credentials once it was discovered that he had declared bankruptcy. A dishonest pastor had abused Leonard and the congregation he served. That corrupt pastor's misery became his predecessor's ministry. Junk happens. And yes, pastors are the cause. But equally devastating to a church is the abuse of the shepherd.

The Inevitable Aftermath

What some church members don't seem to realize is that when you strike the shepherd, the sheep will scatter. Ironically, forcing out a pastor is a two-edged sword with devastating effects for both the pastor and congregation. Even if the pastor wasn't "doing his job," the consequences are far-reaching.

The comeback pastor then arrives on the scene in much the same way a paramedic is called to an accident scene. I've watched enough episodes of "Rescue 911" to know that immediate assessment of the injuries is made. If conscious, the victim is first immobilized. First aid is administered. A collar immobilizes the neck to prevent further spinal injury. Broken legs and arms receive a splint. Only when stabilized is the patient transported via ambulance or care flight to the nearest trauma center. Severely injured persons cannot jump up immediately and return to normal. Tragically, some may be permanently disabled. Others don't survive.

The forced termination of a shepherd can incapacitate the whole flock. All things are possible with God, but that's no guarantee that a severely wounded church will make a comeback. Like a paramedic, a comeback church pastor arrives on the scene to render emergency assistance. Unlike an emergency medical technician, the job doesn't end with the injured safely transported to the nearest emergency room. A comeback pastor stays with the afflicted until the bandages come off. Then comes the rehabilitation therapy. Some have actually witnessed the disappearance of scars.

There is considerable fallout in the aftermath of a forced termination. Weaker members begin to question their loyalty to a church that treats its pastor like that. An exodus of people is often the result, as noted in the examples in this chapter. During my first three years after following Harold Hickman's forced termination, 150 people left the church never to return. You'll not shout "Hallelujah!" when more people are leaving the church than are joining. And yes, you'll struggle to keep from viewing the exodus as a personal affront.

When you find yourself up against the inevitable aftermath, the following survival strategies will enable you to empower a comeback.

1. Receive joyfully what is provided.

If your church asks you to live in its parsonage and you accept the call with the understanding that you will, accept what's provided. When I accepted the Midwest church, our family agreed up front to move into the parsonage, and we loved it. Remember that attitude is everything. Do you prefer to own your own home? Fine. But the time to settle such matters is prior to arrival and with a written understanding of salary and benefits signed by the secretary of the church board, the denominational leader, and you.

2. Refuse to be threatened by the people's love for your predecessor.

As already mentioned, I was Harold Hickman's successor at this Midwest church. And guess what came up at my very first board meeting—the painting that Rev. Hickman would allow only if a portrait of him hung next to it. I listened intently as one board member after another described their love for Bro. Allbright and the family's desire to honor the founder of their church. I know now they were testing to see how I would react. I had already passed the parsonage test.

In a flash of God-inspired diplomacy I said, "You know, hanging a picture in the hallway is kind of impersonal." We were seated around tables in the overflow area outside the sanctuary. "Why don't we make this area where we're sitting into a conference room and library?" I continued. "We could dedicate the room in memory of Bro. Allbright and hang his portrait in this special room." Smiles appeared on every face. Heads nodded in approval. Someone grabbed a calculator and came up with a figure. For about $2,500 we could refurbish the room.

"Pastor," someone interjected, "Bro. Allbright had a special place in his heart for the people of Haiti. Why don't we also build a church there in his memory?"

After more discussion and input, we decided to raise the $7,500 in a special offering. On the day of the memorial offering, more than $8,000 came in to underwrite the expense of the conference room and the cost of building materials for a church in Haiti.

Then I suggested that we have a W. A. Allbright Memorial Day when the conference room was completed. Members of the Allbright family were invited to come for the day at our expense. The family was honored in a fitting celebration of Bro. Allbright's significant contributions. I happily announced that funds had been sent to underwrite the cost of a chapel in the mountains of Haiti in memory of Bro. Allbright.

Be kind to your predecessor. Refuse to be threatened by the people's love for him or her, and, in due time, they will transfer that love and loyalty to you. If, however, you resent the people's love for your predecessor, you may experience forced termination for that blunder. I served as their pastor for seven wonderful years. Lifelong friendships were formed during that time. Once the memorial church in Haiti was completed, the church sent Kaye and me there to dedicate it. Over 40 Haitians were baptized and joined the church that morning. And later at the dedication service, I preached to more than 800 people. Love your predecessor. Big Kingdom business is at stake. If you give a double honor (1 Tim. 5:17), you'll reap lasting rewards.

3. Respect the existing power structure.

Even the corporate world seems to understand that an organization has a culture. I would define culture simply as a way of doing things.

Every church has one, and you must respect the values and group traditions of the people you'll lead. Hans Finzel says, "It's like the glue in plywood—you are not aware of it until you try to take it apart!"[12]

In order to be successful, you must at least respect the fact that every church has certain rules of the game (its own way of doing things). If you run roughshod over the existing structure, upsetting apple carts and changing the rules, you'll create chaos and confusion. Remove one power structure, and a new one will be created. Only the names and faces will change. After Brad left, the struggle for a new power structure began. I can't fully explain how it happens. All I know is that as new leaders emerge, the key influencers come to the forefront, the vacuum is filled, and a whole new way of doing things manifests itself.

4. Reject all advice to take sides.

This is the most difficult task of a comeback pastor. The immediate task in a divided church is to seek some middle ground to which both sides can move. If none can be found or both sides refuse to find some neutral ground they can move to, you'll eventually reach an impasse. Both sides believe their position is right and the other is wrong. A fair amount of posturing and positioning occurs in the start-up days at a divided church. But a comeback pastor must model love and tolerance for everyone. Expect to get shot at from both sides, because even cordiality in conversations with persons on the other side in the church foyer is fodder for those who think you've befriended the enemy.

This happened to me in the early days at one of the churches I pastored. If I so much as greeted the other side before and after the services, somebody accused me of befriending the enemy. They'd say things like "They've gotten to you, haven't they?" I tried to explain that I was the pastor to all the people, and after a while they learned that was true. I refused to play the game. The challenge is to make all the people feel you're on their side, when in truth you're on the Lord's side only.

5. Recognize that hurt people hurt people.

People in pain sometimes do nasty and mean-spirited things. Truly, they know not what they do. Keep your eyes and faith focused on God even in the midst of the pain that hurting people will cause you and others. I actually thought at times that professing Christians hated Brad for what they believed he had done to their church. If the allegations were true, throwing eggs at the parsonage and threatening bodily harm to the pastor's children is an example of how hurt people can hurt people without the slightest twinge of conscience—all because they believed he was wrong and they were right.

6. Rebuild the balance in the bank of trust.

When a church experiences the forced termination of its pastor, whatever balance remains in the bank of trust is reduced practically to zero. Stephen R. Covey uses the metaphor of "The Emotional Bank Account" in *The 7 Habits of Highly Effective People*.[13] The comeback pastor must begin immediately to make major deposits in the bank of trust by doing the following:

   a. Genuinely seeking to understand both sides of an issue
   b. Paying attention to the little kindnesses and courtesies
   c. Keeping commitments and promises
   d. Clarifying expectations
   e. Modeling personal integrity
   f. Apologizing sincerely when a mistake is made

7. Realize that not every battle is worth winning.

Not every issue is worth fighting over. So "Draw your lines in the sand where it counts." You can lose a few battles in the comeback effort and still win the war. You must ask yourself, "Is this a 5-cent or a 500-dollar issue?" The challenge will be to decide whether you've encountered a serious bump in the road or a life-threatening episode.

6   Locusts and Doctrine

In essentials unity, in nonessentials liberality, and in all things charity.
—Augustine

I will repay you for the years the locusts have eaten.
—Joel 2:25

My second comeback church experience could best be described as a "locust year." You may wonder exactly what a locust year is. I wasn't really sure myself until the unforgiving insects blanketed the terrain of my otherwise orderly life. In countries where locusts come intermittently, farmers naturally fear and dread them, because they bring devastation, loss, famine, and even death. Swarming locusts block out the sun with an eerie eclipse of darkness and doom. Locusts devour everything in their path.

In ministry terms a locust year occurs when the bottom falls out. Your hopes of growth and dreams of harvest vanish overnight. All that's left is devastation and decline.

When the ravenous locusts have eaten their fill of crops and have done their worst, they die. Then a marvelous miracle of nature occurs. The carcasses of these deadly destroyers now combine to produce a fertilizer that enriches the soil. Before long an even greater miracle occurs. If a farmer can muster the courage to plant again in spite of his or her previous losses, the year following the greatest destruction, he or she reaps a bountiful harvest. The year following the disaster is a time of bounty, blessing, and tremendous prosperity.

Packed into a sometimes overlooked promise in Joel 2:25 is a diamond of truth for every discouraged, desolate, and devastated comeback pastor on whose church the locusts have descended: "I will restore to you the years that the locust hath eaten" (KJV). God gave me that promise near the end of my second comeback experience while waiting to report on what had been a year of devastating losses.

Locusts, Doctrine, and War

While "locusts" can take on numerous shapes, one of their most prevalent forms is conflict over doctrinal issues. I learned this exactly one week into one of our early pastorates, when locusts appeared on the horizon. I suppose I could have waved them off if I had been willing to compromise the denominational doctrine I had pledged to protect. The beginning of this locust year began when I realized that a substantial number of people held doctrinal beliefs contrary to my own and those of my denomination. These were not the foot-of-the-Cross issues all Christians can agree upon; rather, they involved our denominational core beliefs. I was informed that I would be wise to preach on topics that safely bypassed the issue. That subject was off limits. I had to weigh every word for fear that any theological terminology might be misconstrued. Initial avoidance of the divisive topic temporarily postponed conflict and confrontation. The trouble turned into an ordeal when I refused to change my beliefs and those held by my denomination in order to appease those who disagreed. Regardless of what my church said or the advice I received in handling the situation, the buck stopped with me.

I decided to stand with my denomination regardless of the personal consequences. In terms of leadership, I became the denomination in the eyes of those whose beliefs ran contrary. The conflict began with a rather innocent statement. I had asked several board members to go calling with me to introduce me to the people in the congregation.

One night when Hal pulled his car into the parsonage driveway to drop me off, he turned off the engine and said rather abruptly, "Pastor, before you go in, I want to tell you about my beliefs."

"Oh?" I said. "What beliefs are those?"

Hal responded by describing a belief structure that was not in alignment with our core doctrine. "Now, Pastor," he continued, "you don't have to worry about this; it's private and personal. Just leave us alone, and we'll leave you alone."

Stunned by his disclosure, I simply answered, "Of course, you know, Hal, our denomination does not agree with you in this issue." Nothing further was said.

Unwittingly, I had drawn a line in the sand. I know now that if I had said, "That's OK—do as you please," I could have avoided a lot of grief. Because I didn't give tacit approval, full-scale war broke out. Several months later Hal's group admitted that their intention was to alter our core beliefs.

Three months after my decision to stand with my denomination, the locusts came in hordes. They came in the form of resignations, losses, disruption of families and friendships. The bitterness, tension, and discouragement were almost overwhelming. Opposition to my leadership mounted. Some were even calling for my removal.

Then there were the letters. Some were signed, others unsigned. One day a letter was placed on my desk that caused me great sadness. The note began, "I am sorry to be having to write this letter of resignation . . . and to request my letter of membership." Scott claimed he had lost confidence in the church because it "limited its people." He felt that we were "too wrapped up in doctrine" and had "placed it too high on a pedestal." I understood his anger at the church, but when he prophesied that "the church is doomed under your guidance," I really began to doubt my beliefs and believe my doubts about the stance I had taken.

Scott's negative letter continued, "And I don't believe any other pastor could pull the church out of the gloom it has fallen into." Then he resorted to the favorite tactic of the discontented churchgoer, "I am no longer receiving spiritual food." Scott said he hoped he was wrong concerning the future of the church but forecast that "it is going to be a hard struggle for those who remain to keep it alive." Interestingly, he concluded his letter by stating that my message the previous Sunday had helped him make up his mind. No matter how good you are at preaching and teaching, someone will say, "I'm not getting fed around here." Scott later apologized for the letter, and I readily forgave him. In a gesture of reconciliation, we shook hands, although Scott still expressed confusion about the crisis we found ourselves in.

When Scott left my office that day, I immediately heard raised voices. One of my most ardent supporters, a lady I'll call Claire, saw Scott coming out of my office and jumped to the conclusion that he must be pastor-bashing again. She then proceeded to give him a verbal tongue-lashing. "Why don't you leave?" she fumed. "We don't need troublemakers like you!"

As soon as I learned what Claire had said, I pulled her into my office and confronted her. "What you did was wrong! You just undid the peace I had worked so hard to make with Scott."

Claire would not admit that she was out of line. When you think you're on the right side of an issue, any tactic is deemed justifiable. Later that evening I assured Scott that I did not condone Claire's conduct. Many hours were spent trying to douse the fire this eruption ignited.

The Showdown

The higher-ups in my denomination advised me to publicly confront the remaining rebels and in effect ask them to leave the church. I opted for the less drastic step of contacting all involved personally and privately in order to avoid public humiliation. However, when an adult Sunday School teacher publicly condemned the stance of the church, accusing our leader and me of kicking her friends out of the church, I knew I had to go public. Three days later, another woman resigned her class to "follow the Holy Spirit" and to leave the church because of its "doctrinal intolerance."

I began to sense that some public assurance needed to be given to those whose doctrinal beliefs had been called into question. A fair amount of proselytizing had been going on to get church members to change some of their core beliefs. Even those who held leadership positions in the church were advocating doctrinal beliefs that were alien to the denomination's teaching and doctrine. Members of the errant group became emboldened to witness to their beliefs and to persuade others to support their efforts to remain in the church.

As in any doctrinal dispute, there are people like a man I'll call Ron who selected our denomination because its teachings represented the kind of influence to which he wanted himself and his children exposed. The church's doctrines and practices had proven satisfactory to Ron and his family in all respects and had given them the framework within which their spiritual needs were fully met. The truth is, Ron neither needed nor wanted to pursue any teachings or practices different from those he had found in his own church. Moreover, Ron was distressed that he, and especially his children, were subjected to promotional activities on behalf of contrary beliefs within the walls of his own church and from members of his own congregation. In a letter Ron documented that he had been invited to the errant group's meetings on at least five occasions, and each time the invitation had been extended to him on the premises of the church. These prayer meetings had been discussed in Sunday School classes and in public testimonies in such a way as to suggest that worship, prayer, and fellowship enjoyed at their prayer meetings were "superior" to what was found in the church itself. Ron felt that those involved were using their rights and privileges as members of the church to recruit new persons into their divergent belief system.

With so many questions raised about the church's doctrinal distinctives, I believed the time had come to address the subject in a message. About halfway through my message, Scott was the first to register his disapproval. So much for the understanding I thought we had reached when we met in my office. He stood to his feet and walked out of the choir in full view of the congregation. Several others followed suit. Each stood up, scowled, and stormed out as I continued preaching.

As a result of that one message in which I simply clarified the church's doctrinal stance, ten people requested to be removed from membership. Without a doubt this was the most difficult message I would preach in 30 years of pulpit ministry. Several people registered immediate disapproval of the message, but the majority of members told me I had preached a "masterpiece." My doctrinal stand with the denomination led one man to say, "You have put the church on an irreversible trend toward destruction." He cited at least 25 other people the church stood to lose who were sympathetic with those who had already requested their membership letters.

The stand had been taken. When the dissidents and their sympathizers pressured me to resign, I drew on my courage and declared, "I'm not leaving nor am I seriously considering it." Rumors and innuendoes ran rampant. At one point, Kaye and I were away at a pastors' retreat. When we returned, we caught wind of the rumor that we were leaving. As a show of support, Claire formed the Pastor's Booster Club.

By the time Claire formed that Booster Club, I needed something more like a volcanic explosion to blow me out of the doldrums of depression. Our denomination still requires pastors to give an annual report at their district assembly. Its purpose is accountability, but no one can fully appreciate how agonizing an experience this is when there's little progress to report. Attendance was down. Finances had decreased. Denominational budgets were not paid in full. This was the year we had lost more people than we had gained. But I had to make my report and somehow try to overcome oppressive feelings of failure and inadequacy. Inwardly, I hoped that no one really blamed me for the losses, but the demons of doubt kept shouting in my ears, "You've failed, and soon everyone will know!"

My preacher dad wrote letters of encouragement to his "beleaguered but valiant son" assuring me that he stood beside me—shoulder to shoulder—having confidence in me as a minister and a soldier of the Cross. Probably the best advice he gave me was "Grab your wife and babies and clear out of town every Monday morning. Weekly find diversion of mind and spirit for yourself and your wife." Dad tried desperately to help me get beyond the immediate and "find my wings." He cautioned, "A new situation won't do it. You must find, through prayer and supplication, how to do it right where you are."

I had to fight hard to overcome feelings of failure as the locusts swarmed. Dad would say, "You do well to look at yourself—admit both what you like and don't like about yourself. Acknowledge it and go on." One time he quoted General Dwight Eisenhower when the general was asked to give his basic rule of life to a young officer. Eisenhower said, "Take your job seriously, but not yourself." My dad's encouragement to "drink at the fountains of faith, personal self-improvement, and positive thinking" really helped. He was right: "There are only ulcers and groans and wrinkled brows in negativism." I was beginning to understand why good leaders understand themselves. You must know your strengths and weaknesses before you connect with the people.

The Fulfilled Promise

At long last, the crisis appeared to be over. All the dissenters had moved to other churches, and the remaining members and I were left to try to rebuild after the holocaust.

I've always been fascinated watching workers build a high-rise building. Months seem to go by before the walls go up. Iron workers painstakingly bolt and weld and rivet together a superstructure of steel beams and girders that are securely fastened to a massive concrete foundation. A parable on the necessity of rebuilding after the coming of the locusts evolved as I passed a construction site from day to day. Relationships needed to be mended and rebuilt. Just as building a superstructure without the beams and girders would lead to collapse, so our church would collapse if we didn't pull together for renewed unity.

I pleaded for tolerance, cooperation, mutual understanding, unity, and brotherly love. I urged my leaders to accept each other for who and what they were rather than what each one wished the other person to be. Each person has his or her own idea as to what the church should be. I stressed that we should all quit drawing lines of separation and distance and begin pulling together toward common goals. I recall one impassioned plea to my board in which I said, "Let's emphasize things that unite us rather than things that divide us. Let's build bridges instead of walls. Let's forget past mistakes, failures, and personal shortcomings. Let's forgive. Let's start thinking about and believing what's right about our church."

My final 10 months as pastor of this comeback church were spent building bridges. God had given me a promise that He would restore the years the locusts had eaten (Joel 2:25). I wondered what that meant when support for my leadership continued to dwindle in the remaining six months. Some would always question the way I handled the issue as a man under orders from my superiors. I shed some more blood in those last few months. A petition calling for my removal was threatened. By one estimate there were 20 people who planned to vote against me when my recall vote came up. Those who tried to be loyal expressed the hope that "it wouldn't have to come to a vote." In one woman's words, "A vote would be very divisive." While I was not a forced-out pastor, as detailed in the previous chapter, I did eventually resign. Another opportunity with another congregation posed itself in God's time, and I moved with few if any regrets.

When I left the church, frankly, I was confused. While I've never considered myself infallible, I did believe that God gave me a promise about recovery from the locusts. For a long time after receiving the Joel 2:25 promise, I thought my own ministry would be restored and that I would be the one to lead the comeback.

God had something else in mind. My assignment was preparing the way for my successor, who enjoyed 11 consecutive years of growth. I saw him at a college trustees' meeting, and we talked about the church he had since left after those 11 years of fruitful ministry. He said, "David, your 15 months gave me 11 years of ministry there." Just as the aftermath of a locust invasion serves as fertilizer for next year's crop, so my year of distress proved necessary to prepare the church for major growth. From a low of about 190 in morning worship, the church has grown steadily to nearly 700 today. While God did not use me to orchestrate the comeback, he did use me to prepare the way for comeback. Without the battles I had fought, the church could have been deadlocked.

But that's only one dimension of God's fulfillment of His promise. My youngest daughter, Jennifer, was born during that locust year and was oblivious to most that happened in her first year of life. Twenty years later, she met her husband and was married in that same church. Now 23 years have elapsed since I served there, and Jennifer and her husband are on the pastoral staff at the same church that was "doomed under my leadership." Yes, God can restore and will restore the years that the locusts have eaten. After all, the Church is His and will survive catastrophes as devastating as doctrinal division. Joel 2:25 is clearly a promise of restoration. I am now 25 years removed from that crisis, and God is still fulfilling that promise to the church that some thought I almost killed.

Lessons from a Locust Year Survivor

When a locust year strikes, there's seldom advance warning. The pastor is drawn into the fray whether he or she is prepared or not.

Once the locusts move in, the immediate result is division. Whether the issues involve doctrinal differences or other dissensions, Satan always uses the locusts to trick good people into destructive nitpicking. In this atmosphere Kaye and I became highly susceptible to misunderstanding, injurious criticism, and unreasonable suspicion.

I think the locusts at times arrive upon the breath of Satan and his demons. The devil's goal is to limit effectiveness and annihilate joy. When God's work does not run smoothly and things don't go according to plan, when you find yourself up against the proverbial brick wall, there's a perpetual battle raging in your mind to overcome feelings of failure and futility. Often laypeople are just as frustrated. Without doubt, the battle is a spiritual one. And despite Satan's attacks, our victory is sure; we can count on God to supply the grace to endure.

However, in *Wake Up! You Have a Ministry!* Dave Ray suggests that "Satan may not be in our mess at all. We could be doing such a good job ourselves thwarting our own efforts that Satan has the time to work on someone else."[1] While Satan should be acknowledged, and while we should agree that spiritual warfare is not a myth, we shouldn't blame Satan for every failure or see demons lurking behind every bush. Both pastors and laypeople struggle at times with feelings of failure and frustration, and we tend to blame Satan when we can find no one else. Often this blame game is the last resort to taking responsibility for our own mistakes.

If you're eaten up with locusts and struggling with whom to blame, I hope the mistakes I made and the lessons I learned will help you overcome in your present situation. The following seven suggestions detail some of my own hard-earned wisdom.

1. **Know what you believe and why.** If you're not committed to the church or denomination that ordained you, find one you can agree with that agrees with your understanding of Scripture and experience. Don't try to undermine the faith and practice of others who may differ with you. You must settle in your own mind what you believe and refuse to bend on what you know to be true.

2. **Understand that conflict cannot always be avoided.** You may prefer to be perceived as helpful and friendly and to have everyone like you, but correction is part of a leader's job. Your natural disposition may be to shy away from conflict, but confrontation is often necessary and may lead to positive results.

3. **Acting right is as important as being right.** Often this is as simple as staying calm in the midst of the storm of controversy. In my

case, the controversy centered on a doctrinal argument. The dissenters may try to make the conflict personal, but how you handle the conflict determines whether the outcome is constructive or destructive. Being right is not the goal—being like Jesus is the goal. After you've proved you're right, will the people in the church want the kind of religion you have?

4. **Refuse to demonize believers who differ from you.** There are more than 30,000 denominations in the world, plus tens of thousands of unaffiliated local churches. The potential for doctrinal diversity is almost limitless. Just because a fellow believer disagrees regarding a doctrinal point, that does not mean he or she is full of the devil. The longer I live, the more I find I have something in common with all genuine believers in Jesus Christ.

5. **Never attempt to change another denomination's theology.** Find one that fits what you believe. Christian organizational consultant and author Bob Biehl says that "tennis people" would not be happy in a "bowling church."[2] Each of us has freedom to pick the local church or denomination we choose based on doctrinal, social, vocational, cultural, or ethnic issues. These days tolerance is required for fellow Christians and an appreciation for our multi-faceted Body of Christ. Something else is needed. We need to get to the foot of the Cross, where the ground is level and all believers are equal. For the sake of our Lord, let's agree to agree on Christian essentials and work together to build the Kingdom outside areas of controversy.

6. **Clarify only what is essential.** Don't try to answer every criticism. Go public only when the truth can't be affirmed privately. The rumor mill runs rampant during conflict or controversy. If you try to respond to every criticism, you'll end up chasing the wind. Stand tall and find an appropriate way to speak the truth in love. As someone said, "A closed mouth gathers no foot!"

7. **Do no harm.** A surgeon was once forced to operate on his son in order to save his life. Before entering the surgical suite, he said, "Son, Daddy may hurt you, but I would never intentionally harm you." An inevitable confrontation may initially hurt, but seek always to do no lasting harm. If you can't put out the fire, at least don't fan it.

Will Eva quotes a friend who does not believe that Paul wrote Hebrews. The friend said that if officially asked to recant that belief, he would do so immediately "because it's not worth dying for." He explains,

> There are too many dubious things that we squabble about in our churches. We sometimes seem more willing to kill for them than to die for them. Most of the "truths" are not worthy of the sweat, struggle, and subdivision with which we load them. They become exhausting, damaging distractions that stir up clouds of dust and emit toxic emotional gases that get in our spiritual eyes and lungs so we can't see or breathe deeply the pure air of what really does matter.
>
> On the other hand, there are verities that lie in the fallow soil of our souls, unrecognized for their value. We may give them a certain lip service, but the attention they receive is not proportionate to their almost unbelievable value.[3]

He's right. Not every minor doctrinal point is worth dying for. Only the verities of faith deserve that type of unswayable commitment. It's important, though, to know what you believe and why. And it's equally important to believe God's promises and hold steady when the locusts come to prey on believers.

7 Stick It Out

Never in almost fifty years have I witnessed
so many shepherds who are discouraged and ready to give up.
—Shepherd's Fold Ministries

When the going gets rough, take it on the chin with the rest of us,
the way Jesus did.
—2 Tim. 2:3, TM

A *Los Angeles Times* report in the late 1990s stated, "Roughly
30% to 40% of religious leaders eventually drop out of the ministry."[1]
Livingstone Rasalam, a Christian psychiatrist, believes ministers are
caught in a vicious cycle. He writes,

> Too many pastors are expected to carry out a variety of duties for
> which they are not always prepared to handle—everything from ser-
> mon preparation to administration, or personal counseling. The in-
> evitable mistakes and weaknesses caused by these expectations can
> lead to insecurity, making a pastor feel like a failure. Frustration be-
> gins to mount, causing more mistakes and finally, burnout. It is a
> self-perpetuating cycle![2]

The Big Five Stress Points

Evangelist Norman Moore states, "After 21 years in full-time evangelism, I have observed three common stress factors for the pastor and
spouse: Unrealistic expectations, unfair criticism, and inappropriate financial compensation."[3] In addition to Moore's three points, I have also
witnessed member migration and consumer mentality to be contributing
factors in pastoral stress. Since unrealistic expectations topped Moore's
list, let's delve into that one first.

1. Unrealistic Expectations

The task of a comeback church pastor is fraught with ever-expand-
ing expectations. Exacting work has been around for about as long as

there have been pastors. Augustine, the famed North African bishop, around A.D. 400 described the pastor's work like this: "Disturbers are to be rebuked, the low spirited to be encouraged, the infirm to be supported, objectors confuted, the treacherous guarded against, the unskilled taught, the lazy aroused, the contentious restrained, the haughty repressed, litigants pacified, the poor relieved, the oppressed liberated, the good approved, the evil borne with, and all are to be loved."[4] Even then, the pastor's task was formidable.

The Alban Institute has identified 76 different roles for the pastor. At the web site of Shepherd Care authors suggest, "Ministers are often viewed as being so many things—Super Hero, Suffering Servant, Voice of God, Social Coordinator, Holy Judge, Miracle Worker, Seer, Charity Organizer, even as God—and with each one of these views comes expectations that can be confounding."[5] Being Christ's servant today equals being superhuman—even more so for the comeback pastor.

The boundaries are ever expanding as radical changes and unreasonable expectations seem to rule the day. Pastor John Schmidt in an article entitled "Putting Them in Their Place" cites the reason why so many are being catapulted out of the ministry:

> The pastoral role moved from simple shepherding to being CEO, CFO, resident lawyer, visionary, program manager, God's perfect counselor on all matters, fidelity fixer, facilities superintendent, perpetual committee member, human resources director, successful fundraiser, supervisor, politician, spiritual example, masterful preacher, artful teacher, community leader, welfare administrator, contractor, organizational appeaser, and too often people-pleaser. Ah, and oh yes, perfect spouse, and perfect parent with perfect children in the perfect home.[6]

In *Holy Humor* Cal and Rose Samra share the profile of a perfect pastor:

> He preaches exactly 15 minutes. He condemns sin but never upsets anyone. He works from 8:00 A.M. to midnight and is also a janitor. He makes $50 a week, wears good clothes, buys good books, drives a good car, and gives about $50 weekly to the poor. He has a burning desire to work with teenagers and spends all of his time

with senior citizens. The perfect pastor smiles all the time with a straight face because he has a sense of humor that keeps him seriously dedicated to his work. He makes 15 calls daily on parish families, shut-ins, and the hospitalized. He spends all of his time evangelizing the unchurched and is always in his office when needed. If your pastor does not measure up, simply send this letter to six other parishes that are tired of their pastor, too. Then bundle up your pastor and send him to the church at the top of the list. In one week, you will receive 1,643 pastors, and one of them should be perfect.

Finally, the authors caution, "Have faith in this letter. One church broke the chain and got its old pastor back in less than three weeks."[7] In his book *Today's Pastors,* George Barna states,

The pastor knows what is expected of him . . .
- Live an exemplary life.
- Be available at all times to all people for all purposes.
- Lead the church to grow numerically.
- Balance wisdom with leadership and love.
- Teach people the deeper truths of the faith in ways that are readily applicable in all life situations.
- Be a committed family man who demonstrates what it means to be the spiritual head of the family, a lover of one woman, and a positive role model for children.
- Keep pace with the latest trends and developments in church life.
- Build significant relationships with members of the congregation.
- Represent the church in the community.
- Grow spiritually.
- Run the church in a crisp, professional, business-like manner without taking on a cold, calculating air.[8]

The multiplicity of expectations has increased the pressure upon today's pastors to suffocating levels. Is it any wonder, then, that "pastors are the single most occupationally frustrated group in America?"[9] The Barna Research Group's 1993 survey of ministers' wives revealed that 53 percent of ministers' wives believe unrealistic expectations to be the biggest problem they face in ministry. As Alan Heller reminds in a *Focus on the Family* article, "Elder boards, finance committees, church members, unsaved neighbors, local media, family members, and denominational leadership exert unique pressures on the pastor's heart and mind. Yet none will deep-six his life more quickly and thoroughly than those within his marriage."[10]

Norman Moore told me about a pastor's wife who was heavily involved in her Saturday home responsibilities of laundry, house cleaning, and grocery shopping. She received a phone call from a lady in the church who impulsively pressured the pastor's wife to help her make numerous phone calls to promote attendance at a church event that presumably she was in charge of. When the pastor's wife explained that she could not drop everything and make the calls the woman was imposing, her reply was, "It sounds like you're busy; that stands for 'buried under Satan's yoke.'" Then she abruptly hung up.[11]

Hugh Prather suggests that expectations are "an enslaving judgment we make of each other." They are often "so far off the mark of reality or possibility that they drive wedges between people who formerly had fine relationships before one (or five) of them got carried away with an impossible ideal." As a solution he recommends, "Expectations, like cataracts, must be removed because there is no way around them."[12]

William Moore studied 341 clergy from 36 denominations and 43 states and discovered that "unrealistic expectations are a major factor in pastor burnout."[13] Long hours of work coupled with unending demands leave open the doors of discontent. Comeback pastors possess an "inner agitator" that "is actually an inner antagonist—an accuser—who arouses fears of failure," to remind us "of unfulfilled obligations, and saturates thoughts with blame"[14]—that "a task-master within" prods, nudges, and drives us. Laypeople tell me that this is a plight that affects both sides of the altar. Perhaps this is less a laity problem or ministry problem and more of a lack of focus on Christ. As long as pastors or laypeople are focused on what they expect from each other, they aren't focused on Christ and will not win souls. Add to this the unrealistic expectations of a few misguided, dysfunctional, or troubled people, and "the resulting bondage produces a dismal ministry" if not burnout and migration out of ministry altogether.[15] I tell my pastors when I install them to do their best and leave the rest to God, realizing that not all expectations can be met. If you're a comeback church pastor, you'll easily work 60 to 80 hours a week and still face the reality of unfinished work.

John Schmidt describes "the vast array of parishioners" a pastor must serve today. "While the majority of believers are honest and loving, there is a growing company in the discontented category." This "modern contingent of last day human beings are placing new stresses on godly leaders." Some of the people in our churches come from dysfunctional environments and struggle with the long-term effects of abuse, neglect, and hurt. Schmidt concludes, "Without God's healing hand certain ones become victims who look for revenge on the leaders of society. Pastors are sitting ducks."[16]

It is important to understand that suffocating expectations are control issues. Norman Moore says, "When a demanding controller, who insists on having his or her own selfish way, lobs grenades of [unfair] criticism at the pastor or spouse, the results are added stress and discouragement."[17] These homegrown hypocrites are adept at devouring those in positions of power with no thought of living the life of Christ on a daily basis. These new Pharisees blanket their own sins in a cloak of religiosity and are quick to judge and are skilled at group manipulation. Believe me—you'll encounter them in the course of a comeback experience. You may empathize with their internal pain, but you may bear the brunt of their uncontrolled anger when you cannot give them their way.

2. Unfair Criticism

Let's face it: pastors and laity receive unwarranted and often unjustifiable criticism. I'm sure you've heard the old adage that there are just two days in which the average person is free from criticism—the day he or she is born and the day he or she dies. Criticism can extinguish enthusiasm and douse joy more quickly than just about anything I can think of. We know how good words fortify and bless us, but nothing knocks the props from under our confidence like unfair and undeserved criticism. Dennis Rainey in *Pulling Weeds, Planting Seeds* tells of the spiteful relationship between Winston Churchill and Lady Astor; they made no attempt to hide their contempt for one another. One day Lady Astor said to Churchill, "Mr. Prime Minister, if you were my husband I'd poison your drink." Not to be outdone, he sharply replied, "Well, if you were my wife, I'd drink it."

On another occasion Lady Astor found that Churchill had been drinking a little too freely. "Mr. Prime Minister," she scolded, "I perceive you are drunk!" He smiled and wryly replied, "Yes, Lady Astor, and you are ugly. But tomorrow I shall be sober."[18]

Robert Schuller once said on a television broadcast that words can be "bullets, bombs, or blessings." Unfair criticism, if not a bullet or bomb, is what John Stott calls "the devil's talk," and both pastors and laypeople should not listen to it. "Whether it be lies or propaganda, slander or gossip, filth or insults," or even "anonymous letters," Stott says, "we should not take seriously the criticisms of a correspondent who lacks the courage to disclose his or her identity."[19] Anonymous letters are rude and upsetting. Some pastors open a letter and immediately check for a signature. If they see none, they throw it in the trash. Me? I'm a little too curious. I've peeked. And whenever I have, it has hurt.

Joseph Parker, minister of the City Temple in London at the end of the 19th century, was hit by a piece of paper thrown at him by a lady in the gallery as he climbed into his tall pulpit one Sunday morning. Picking it up, he found that it contained a single word: "fool." In a flash of inspiration Dr. Parker commented, "I have received many anonymous letters in my life. Previously they have been a text without a signature. Today, for the first time, I have read a signature without a text!"[20] Keep your sense of humor intact, and laugh at some silly criticisms.

When giving criticism. Before criticizing others, ask yourself these questions: Is it true? Is it necessary? Is it helpful? Is the timing right? What you say may be true, but is it necessary? How helpful will your words be? Unnecessary, trivial criticisms can and should be avoided. True criticism given at the wrong time can be devastating. An unknown author prayed, "Lord, give me eyes that I might see, lest I as people will, should pass someone's Calvary and think it is just a hill."

When receiving criticism. The difficult part—and I'm still a work in progress in this regard—is to recognize the wisdom or "friendly advice" in some criticism that could lead me to make positive changes. The trick is to hear what your critic is actually saying without being discouraged, detracted, or destroyed by it. Victor M. Parachin in an article in *Ministry* suggests, "People who are intimidated by their critics live timid, hesitant, and invisible lives."[21]

Faultfinders are quick to point out the negative and slow to see the positive. Do they have facts to back up their faultfinding? Or do they just lump facts and opinions together? If the critic uses excessive generalities or is overly negative, his or her conclusions may be invalid. But if what the critic says is logical, and he or she makes positive suggestions you might be able to implement, you might become a better person to heed the advice. As Gordon MacDonald says, "There is a kernel of truth in every critique. Look for it, and you'll be a better (person)."[22]

How does criticism affect you and your work? Does it rob you of your initiative and creativity? How does it affect you emotionally? If you're so emotionally fragile that you nearly fall to pieces every time you hear an unfair criticism, you're in for a bumpy ride in a comeback church assignment.

3. Inappropriate Financial Compensation

With all our earthly goods loaded into a U-Haul, Kaye and I began our journey from seminary to the Spacecoast community of central Florida. Behind us we pulled our 1969 Mustang. Kaye rode shotgun with our six-month-old daughter, Sonya, strapped between us in her car seat. Filled with the hopes, aspirations, and idealism of recently graduated seminarians, we began our career in vocational ministry.

There were fewer than 50 members in the congregation, but that was 48 more than the two-member congregation I had been offered in Cedarburg, Wisconsin. And it was warmer.

My starting salary was a whopping $100 per week, in part subsidized by our denominational district. The church raised a total of $18,000 that first year, $6,000 of which went to pay the mortgage. Out of the remaining $13,000 my salary and all other expenses, including maintenance, ministry, and, of course, denominational budgets had to be paid. The church did its best, and besides, I thought ministry was not about money anyway.

I certainly didn't enter vocational ministry with any thought that wealth would result. And God forbid that I should ever complain. I made that mistake in the presence of a wealthy layman who scolded, "You chose your calling, so don't complain." The implication was that if I wanted to get in on the world's gravy I should have chosen a more lucrative profession. The subtle message was that I would get mine in heaven —he would take all he could get here. But *I* really didn't choose this vocation. Jesus said, "You didn't choose me, remember; I chose you, and put you in the world to bear fruit, fruit that won't spoil" (John 15:16 TM).

The difference is more than semantics: God chose me and ordained me to serve Him as a vocational minister. If you don't feel that way about your calling, you will not last for a lifetime in ministry.

While serving Christ full-time as a minister isn't about money, those of us in vocational ministry deserve to be fairly compensated and earn our living from the gospel. The apostle Paul argued for this "right" in 1 Cor. 9, although he did not exercise this claim (9:12). In those early days I readily identified with Paul, who wrote, "Woe to me if I do not preach the gospel!" (1 Cor. 9:16). "Yes, even if compelled to do so without financial support," he was stating, "I must preach." Paul may have been the first bivocational preacher. In the words of another version, "If I proclaim the Message, it's not to get something out of it for myself. I'm *compelled* to do it, and doomed if I don't! If this was my own idea of just another way to make a living, I'd expect some pay. But since it's not my idea but something solemnly entrusted to me, why would I expect to get paid?" (1 Cor. 9:16, TM). I confess, however, that I entered this profession fully expecting to receive my livelihood from full-time vocational ministry.

A pastor friend said that when he was an evangelist and revival meetings weren't coming and his income was nil, someone chided, "Aren't you living by faith?"

"Sure," my friend replied, "but have you ever tried to eat faith?"

Unfortunately, many faithful servants not only live by faith—they eat by faith.

Pastoral compensation continues to be a source of pressure and frustration. We're not in ministry for the money, and the people we serve know that. Laypeople also know the cost of living for housing, clothing, transportation, groceries, education, and saving for retirement. Pastors are expected to do all of these things for less. Perhaps this accounts for the fact that many Protestant pastors are bivocational. This in turn may be why the typical pastor devotes only about a quarter of his or her time to personal ministry. If this results in a decrease in the church program and triggers member migration to other churches that have more to offer, the pastor is sometimes blamed for the weakened condition of the church.

Total compensation has improved in the last decade, but few ministers have shared in the boom times of the 90s and early 21st century. If a male pastor is not bivocational, his wife has joined the ranks of working women to help balance the budget. Many good people continue to respond to the call with no thought of the personal sacrifice. In "The Pastor's Weekly Briefing," H. B. London Jr. reminded today's pastors, "You are the survivors!" The article cited a statistic from *Leadership* that revealed, "The average *total* compensation for solo pastors: $37,793; for senior pastors: $53,607."[23] Those statistics certainly don't compare with my denomination's average of a little over $28,000. The subtle impression is that this may account for why so many drop out of the ministry. However, 60 percent to 70 percent of pastors *do* survive and often at a less than subsistence level because, like Paul, the calling compels them.

Many pastors joyfully serve for low pay or in some cases no pay, because, like the apostle Paul, they gladly do so for the privilege of proclaiming the gospel. Inability by a small church to pay a living wage is one thing. Stinginess when more could be paid is another matter entirely. When a church or its leaders are tight, cheap, narrow, and small with their pastor, this contributes to unnecessary stress, pressure, and frustration for the pastor and spouse.

If you are one of those pastors who has served in small churches for most of your career, you may wonder how you'll make ends meet when you retire. There are no guarantees, of course, but I'd like to think that heaven takes notice of sacrificial service. A pastor I know has served small congregations for most of his ministerial career. In his 50s he and his wife scraped together what little savings they had to purchase a modest retirement home from a widow in a former church. She gave them an affordable rate of interest, and with his spouse working part-time, they managed to make their payments on time. Just weeks before retirement, the widow died. When her estate was settled, the heirs informed the pastor that they were forgiving the debt on the house. Though I can't tell you how, I believe God will take care of those who take up the towel of Christian service and minister in Jesus' name.

4. Member Migration

People will leave your church. This phenomenon of "member migration" has always been with us. Vance Havner wrote in *Hearts Afire*, "Too many restless Christians today move from church to church, preacher to preacher. . . ever learning but never able to come to a knowledge of the truth . . . always laying foundations but never building thereon." Havner called these folks "hypodermic saints," living on shots of religious excitement instead of growing normally by food, rest, and exercise. He concluded, "Unless some stabilization is mixed with our salvation, we are going to have a generation of popcorn Christians, popping all over the place."[24]

Pastors may be just as guilty. We tend to condemn the laity for such practices, but honestly, I was guilty of the same malady. My average tenure across 24 years of pastoral ministry in comeback churches was 3.4 years. The shortest stint was 15 months, and the longest was only seven years. I see now that I grew restless and disappointed many parishioners when I seemed to abandon them. This is a problem with both laypeople and pastors.

My first experience of member migration came when 30 willful people and about 55 sympathizers left our church because of denominational doctrine, as detailed earlier. I resigned after 15 months rather than face the prospect of being voted out. My next assignment was in St. Louis, where I followed a forced-out pastor, also discussed in another chapter. Over the course of my first three years at that church, 150 disheartened people went elsewhere despite my best efforts to keep them tied to the church. Next, we took a church in Illinois, where 200 members moved due to economic decline. In my last comeback effort, 500 people migrated out of the seriously divided congregation in search of peace and unity. The member migration finally slowed to a trickle when, on one Sunday, 65 people walked out, never to return.

Yes, I know the heartache of member migration. Take it from one who's been there: If your sense of well-being is tied to the number of people you're able to retain in a difficult comeback assignment, the pressure is unbearable. If you're leading a comeback effort, your first challenge is to halt the decline. You must divert attention away from decline. As I said before, this may be as simple as taking down the attendance scoreboard or refraining from publishing attendance and finance figures that reflect serious, ongoing decline. The less you accent decline, the better. People don't need their noses rubbed in the reduction. Reporting minuses only feeds the fire of negativity and fosters pessimism.

When I started out in ministry, a little piece of me died every time a member migrated, even for a legitimate reason like a job transfer. This is partly because I have a shepherd's heart. I cared for every person ever entrusted to my care. To let a member go was difficult. As I matured, however, I learned that I could not tie people to me. The Kingdom is best served when we tie our people to Christ. Eventually, I accepted that people leaving was not an indication of failure on my part. But honestly, at times I may have been at fault. I know I made mistakes. As mentioned earlier, without fail, no matter how good I thought I was, someone would say, "I'm just not being fed around here." Eventually I realized what they meant. They were *fed up!* If you happen to be leading a church in decline to a comeback, you must come to terms with member migration. You can't control this ministry hazard. Member migration has probably been around for centuries—at least for as long as there have been multiple churches to choose from. I wonder if our forebears hated this ministry peril as much as we do.

5. Consumer Mentality

A church for me and mine. Closely related to member migration is the pressure caused by the abandonment of sacrifice and loyalty in favor of consumerism and a spectator sport mentality. In *Pastors at Risk*, the authors describe church members as "wild geese on the move—not leaving the church, just moving to another local congregation."[25] Loyalty seems to depend on whether *my* needs are met. Regardless of the factors that may contribute to a sharp decline in attendance or finances, people freely go shopping for another church that has more to offer—often to escape responsibility. This has escalated the pressure on today's pastors to offer a smorgasbord of programs and ministries to satisfy the super-market mentality of people. Neither the denominational label nor doctrinal stance of the particular church is at issue. The bottom line is this: Does your church meet the needs of *me* and *mine*? If it doesn't, even faithful attendees may move on without warning to a full-service church that can meet those needs.

Before we cast the first stone against the laity on this issue, how many large-church pastors will take a smaller church or a struggling church? Don't pastors expect to move up the ladder when they take the next church? Aren't they interested in "the next church" meeting their needs on a bigger scale and offering more programs for their families as well as a "better package"—stuff that will meet more of their needs and make them look better in the ministry arena? I mentioned earlier in the book that some of my colleagues thought I was nuts when I left a booming church to take a smaller, struggling one. I began to believe them when we lost $10,000 on the sale of our house.

Some of our members move on for legitimate reasons.

For instance, a woman who is divorced told me that she attended a large church in southern Texas about 20 years ago. She was divorced and struggling. When she had surgery, not one church person came to assist her. She told me it was because she was divorced and was "looked down upon." She now attends another church and doesn't have a good opinion of her former denomination. Frankly, I can't say that I blame her.

While I do believe that some laymen have adopted the consumer mindset, sometimes laymen change churches because they are wounded and are desperate for somebody in a church to show them unconditional love and God's mercy and grace instead of judgment. Before we categorize *all* laypeople who leave us as consumers, we should probably take a closer look. They might be so spiritually wounded they can barely walk, let alone think in terms of ministering to others.

The walking wounded need unconditional love. That will never go out of style. I can guarantee you that when a person feels loved, he or she will not be lured away by bigger and better programs. If you pastor a small church and are despairing that you can't compete with the big church across town—love people! Christ's unconditional love never goes out of style. For every layperson with a consumer mentality, there's a person in the neighborhood who isn't looking for flare and programs but is simply looking for love. If you focus on the shortcomings of laypeople, you'll miss major opportunities for outreach, ministry, and soul winning.

I'm sure that George, described in chapter one, who was collecting cans and came into our church that Sunday, wouldn't have stayed a minute—despite the programs—if he hadn't felt loved. George wasn't looking for fancy programs. He was in need of love and soda pop cans. The Sunday School class, which incidentally collected cans for him, was not a fancy program, but it was what he needed! The class supplied what he needed and thus reached a family for Christ. Any church can strive to do that regardless of its size.

A church for those not potty trained. People often migrate to where the action is. The competition is fierce, and more often than not, the small-church pastor ends up feeling like a big loser when he or she can't offer the same smorgasbord of ministries a megachurch can offer. In over-churched cities, churches trade members back and forth, and we call it growth. Become a church that cares about hurting people, and your church—regardless of its size—can be used by God to transform lives.

People who choose a church on the basis of what the church does for them are so focused on self-fulfillment and personal happiness that they may abandon their church at the slightest whim. In one of the churches I served, one couple left over potty training. Our children's department had instituted a promotion policy for toddlers based on whether the child was potty trained. If the child wasn't, the parents were asked to change their child's dirty diaper between Sunday School and the morning worship service. Most parents complied. Not this couple. They opted to shop for another church where someone would change diapers for them. I still think there were other issues with these dear folks. They weren't troublemakers. They were actively involved in the children's department. Maybe other incidents had soured them on our church, and the diaper changing was the last in a long line of irritations.

The truth is, there are folks out there who are nothing more than adult children. They need us to wrap our arms around them, but they may not tell us the true reason why we've failed to meet their needs. We must learn to look past their negativity to their wounds. This is another in a long line of learning experiences that sometimes seem unending. While I do believe that there are shallow people in churches who seem to be infants, I also believe that these very people who cause the most heartache and maybe are jumping from one church to the next are just like you and me—in desperate need of unconditional love.

When a family throws down its marbles and leaves as the couple did over potty training, it will rip your heart out if you care. When pastors have a "them versus us" mentality, they'll look down on their laity, causing walls and no growth. If you view your people as "consumers," they'll sense your arrogant attitude. But when there's a decided lack of arrogance from the pastor, the laypeople will often respond in a miraculous way.

I have friends who have been on the receiving end of pastoral arrogance. Did they cause problems? No. They just kept paying their tithe, kept up faithful attendance, kept smiling and supporting, and put up walls—because they sensed that their pastor looked down on them and couldn't be fully trusted.

If the laity doesn't fully trust their pastor, they won't be inspired to invite their hurting friends to church. They have the legitimate fear that the pastor would project the same arrogance to their friends and end up driving them farther away from Jesus rather than drawing them into the Kingdom. Between arrogant pastors and consumer-minded laity, there's enough blame to go around.

A church for takers, not givers. As we know the consumer mentality prompts people to change churches for a variety of reasons: better children's programs, more entertaining music, larger facilities, more convenient parking, exciting preaching, or more energetic services. The pressure to outperform your competitors is immense. Norman Moore is right: "Although every church could improve somewhere, to impose idealistic comparisons often contributes unnecessary pressure [upon pastors and spouses]."[26] Is it too cynical to say that we've become a church of takers rather than givers? Takers believe the church exists to satisfy their wants and wishes. The remedy for this mindset on both sides of the altar is the Jesus attitude (Phil. 2:5). To coin the phraseology of John F.

Kennedy, perhaps we should say, "Ask not what your church can do for you, but what you can do for your church."

All of these stress factors contribute to occupational frustration and perhaps burnout. Our profession has been characterized as more stress-filled than a doctor dealing with a terminal illness. But unlike the doctor who walks away from the situation when he leaves the room, the pastor normally has emotional links to those being helped. Is there any way to prevent clergy burnout? The following are some techniques that have helped me.

Eight Maneuvers for Surviving Clergy Burnout

1. Be attentive to the spiritual disciplines.

Learn to depend on divine resources. God has all the power we need to accomplish our work for Him. We must stay close to our Leader and Provider. We can't do that unless we develop a daily quiet time with the Lord. Devotional reading of Scripture—not just to find sermons—must become your wellspring for spiritual nurture. There is a place of quiet rest alone in the presence of our loving Lord.

Read good books. Leaders are readers. And yes, read something non-religious every now and then. Your brain needs an occasional detour. Remember that you're cultivating your mind and soul. Journaling is a helpful way to stay focused in prayer. Guard your heart. Continually apply preventative measures to your inner world to keep yourself spiritually and emotionally well. Trying to serve God in your own strength and in your own way is "off-center leadership." Rely on divine resources. They're available from God, who promised sufficient power to accomplish significant work. Stay close to Him. He will provide daily spiritual refreshment.

2. Religiously protect a weekly day off.

Recharge your mental and spiritual batteries with recreation and rest. You must give your soul time to catch up. If you're like me, on Mondays I usually suffer from the effects of adrenaline depletion, what pastoral psychologist Archibald Hart calls "post-adrenaline depression." I didn't understand why on Mondays, after a grueling day of two or three services, I was so irritable, impatient, and non-communicative at home.

Adrenaline depletion is real. Remember that you're in ministry for the long haul. You need some down time. Maintain pace and balance to protect your spiritual and emotional health.

In my fifth comeback church, Norm and Marilyn gave me a key and allowed me to take a "Friday Sabbath" afternoon away from the office and demands of ministry in the privacy of their home. I read, prayed, and meditated. Honestly, the most refreshing thing I did on those Friday afternoon retreats was to take a good nap in Norm's big easy chair in the den. Comeback pastors need to take a weekly Sabbath, even if, like mine, it was for only a few hours on a Friday afternoon.

3. Establish a network of supportive relationships.

Find a friend or confidant (perhaps from clergy of another denomination) who will give you personal and spiritual support. Cultivate a same-gender prayer or accountability partner. Arrogance says, "I can make it on my own. I don't need anyone else." We really do need each other. Don't take a wrong turn toward burnout by being a "lone ranger" in ministry. God doesn't expect you to minister alone, so be on the lookout for supportive relationships. Find or create a regular support group of colleagues and friends.

4. Enrich your life at home.

Take advantage of time together with your spouse and family. Early in ministry I learned that the first obligation of ministry is to show your people a good marriage. Even in a comeback assignment, your family is your number-one ministry assignment. A good marriage is a gift we give to ourselves and to our churches. Your family is next in priority to God and is a gift from Him. Feed faith to your children, not negativism and distress. Remember that your light is always shining at home. Your family observes firsthand your reactions to the pressures of a comeback effort. In our comeback challenges, my daughters observed their mom and dad in action and reaction. I thank God that both are committed Christians today.

I would caution you to avoid giving your wife and children the leftovers of your mental and emotional energy. The comeback experience is time-consuming and requires indefatigable energy. If you stumble in the door night after night so spent that you have nothing left for your wife or kids, you're in a destructive pattern. We must set limits for ourselves if we're to avoid burnout.

5. Exercise.

We hold our bodies and nervous systems in trust from God and should treat His property well. I used to run for my life. Now in my mid-50s, I walk. I would rather eat than exercise, but I grab myself by the scruff of the neck and hit the pavement two or three times a week. If you don't like to walk alone, walk with your spouse. Plan a recreational break in your weekly schedule. A healthy body does wonders for mental and emotional well-being. Stamina is increased when the body is in good shape.

In our younger days, my wife and I play golf together regularly. Golf is good exercise and relaxing as long as I don't take myself too seriously or make the mistake of trying to be Kaye's golf coach. This sport has been great for our relationship as well. If you don't like golf, develop a hobby or sport or some other interests outside the church. Recreation and exercise are essential coping strategies for pastors in the pressure cooker of the comeback church experience.

6. Limit the number of clinging vines.

The key to avoiding burnout is to strike a healthy balance between those who exhaust you and those who invigorate you. This helpful advice came to me as I read Gordon MacDonald's book *Restoring Spiritual Passion*. Being with people is exhausting in itself. The people you spend time with will either deplete you or replenish you. As mentioned earlier, "very draining people" will exhaust you and "ultimately create a climate in which no one will want to serve in leadership capacities."[27] So surround yourself with big-thinking people—people who stretch you, people whose faith is contagious and bolstering.

7. Avoid "the deep water training program."

Your ministry can easily become like an "overstuffed glove compartment," meaning that you're on call 24/7/365, and your schedule takes over your life. This pace will wear you out. Ask appropriate questions before you make another commitment:

- Can I attend the number of meetings expected?
- Do I possess the training and expertise called for?

If not, you might unwittingly be entering the "deep water training program," in which you sink or swim on your own. You might consider making a conditional commitment. Try a job on for size to see if you're really suited for a long-term commitment. Avoid over-involvement that may cause you to lose touch with your divine Resource. If you're too busy to pray, you'll sink on your own. Realize that the nature of the comeback assignment requires that some important things will have to go undone. Make certain the important things that go undone are not the most important things.

8. Laugh a lot.

You can't laugh and develop an ulcer at the same time. Laughter has tremendous healing power. And Proverbs says it's good medicine. Laughter is a form of physical exercise. It causes huffing and puffing, accelerates the heart rate, raises blood pressure, speeds up breathing, increases oxygen consumption, exercises the muscles of the face and stomach, and relaxes muscles not involved in laughing. It stimulates the liver, stomach, pancreas, spleen, and gall bladder. Through laughter the entire body gets an invigorating lift.

Ted Lee has been a close friend since our days in seminary. He calls me regularly, and he makes me laugh. He has been known to leave some of the most hilarious messages on my office answering machine. Laugh at yourself. Laugh at your mistakes. Surround yourself with people who laugh. Whatever you do, don't take yourself too seriously.

At a recent denominational meeting, Saturday morning came, and we had not taken a break from pastor's reports. I excused myself and edged my way through the maze of cords and percussion equipment onstage to a restroom in the green room, yes, wearing my lapel mike. Well, I forgot to turn off my microphone. The clink of the toilet seat was the first sound heard by the delegation. Then came the sound of a rushing mighty flow. A visitor to the sound booth interrupted the sound technician. He dove for the control, killing the mike just before I flushed.

The funny thing was that I had no clue what had happened. When I returned to the sanctuary, many people started laughing. Obviously they had not had their mirth control pills! I thought they were laughing because I couldn't wait for a break, so I said when I sat down, "At least I feel better!" Still oblivious to what they had heard in living sound, a couple of notes came to the desk empathizing with my being such a good sport. *What were they talking about?* One of our pastors was walking slowly to the microphone, so I started counting, 1001, 1002, 1003 . . . He turned, smiled, and said, "Splish-splash to you, Doctor!" Not until then did I realize what had happened. My face turned beet red, and I crawled under the table.

The next morning when I awakened, I looked out the window and spotted something in my front yard under the tree. There sat a commode with the lid up. A computer desktop microphone had been attached to the lid with the crook of the neck pointed into the bowl. The pranksters had imprinted on the lid the core values I had emphasized in a previous meeting: "We are Christian . . . holiness . . . missional . . ." And then was added "urinal!" Since then, no one has claimed the commode, and people all over the denomination have had a good laugh. My friend Ted once left a message on my answering machine in which he sang me a little song: "Tinkle, tinkle, little star. How I wonder where you are!" Now do you see why it's best not to take yourself too seriously?

9. Let God measure your success.

In the midst of the struggle, feelings of worthlessness may push you to the limits. Discouragement may put you down quicker than anything. The late Charles Strickland once told of his first days as a missionary to South Africa. He got a tent and started holding revival meetings. He preached 17 revivals in the same tent at the same location before he had his first convert. He became very discouraged and lonely. His supervisor, Hardy Powers, sent him a letter of encouragement during this time and asked, "What are you doing?" Dr. Strickland was so discouraged that he sent the letter back with the word "Nothing!" scrawled across the page in big letters.

That brought an immediate and rather harsh response from his supervisor. In his follow-up letter, Dr. Powers reminded the young missionary that the church had sent him there to do a job and that he could not come home until the job was completed. "You might as well make the best of it," Dr. Powers wrote. "No replacement will be sent!" Not necessarily an encouraging message, but the missionary held on, and after the 17th revival, the break came. Discouragement and too much stress could cause you to make the same mistake. Don't listen to the demons telling you, "Your work is fruitless . . . your ministry is in vain . . . you have no reason to go on!" Your success yardstick is flawed when you're discouraged. Do your best, and leave the success to God. Best of all, you have not been left to fend for yourself.

10. Pray for a leader-mentor like Paul.

Only God can keep you going when external influences say it's time to quit. God often uses leader-mentors like the apostle Paul to encourage us. Paul's protégé, Timothy, was in a difficult assignment at Ephesus when he received an encouraging letter from his overseer. From his prison cell, Paul inspired his "son in the faith," who struggled with timidity and his youthfulness, to "throw [himself] into this work for Christ. Pass on what you heard from me . . ." (2 Tim. 2:1-2, TM). Paul energized Timothy to "endure hardship" (v. 5). "It's what I'm sitting in jail for right now. . . . That's why I stick it out here—so that everyone God calls will get in on the salvation of Christ in all of its glory" (2:9-10, TM). Then Paul pointed his son in the faith to "a trustworthy saying" (v. 11)—"If we stick it out with him, we'll rule with him" (v. 12, TM). Every Timothy needs a Paul.

In my last comeback effort I seemed to need weekly, if not daily, encouragement to persevere. Just when I most seemed to need encouragement, the telephone would ring. One day David Spittal, a former parishioner and now president of Central Wesleyan College, tracked me down. The piercing ring of my car phone startled me to attention. "How are you doing?" David asked. "You've been on my mind for days, and I have to know—what's going on?" Sensing frustration in my voice, David encouraged me to be strong in the Lord despite the impossible circumstances that drained my spirit. Then he prayed for me. I drove on refreshed, praising the Lord for fresh comfort from a caring colleague. David was a Paul to this Timothy.

Others wrote me letters of encouragement as I fought spiritual warfare. I'll always cherish the "crow letter" I received from Paul Cunningham. He wrote, "When I left the office for lunch today, I noticed probably at least a hundred crows on the ground and perched on top of the building. It appeared they were all looking for something dead to eat. They came to the wrong place, for there is life in this building, the very life of Christ himself, who extends His hands through His helpers who work here to reach around the world in His name." He continued: "I sense the crows have been waiting for some time to feast on your church, but I am confident that they will be disappointed. Christ is into building His church, not killing it. And I continue to believe that somehow, some way, new life is going to burst forth from *your* congregation."

Dr. Paul's Six Handles to Hold On To

The following wisdom came from Dr. Cunningham's crow letter to an embattled servant in the throes of a church in conflict. Recalling them now brings fresh encouragement never to quit when serving in a difficult comeback assignment.

1. Believe that Christ has the power to change hearts and your situation. Dr. Cunningham's letter came before Christmas, that special season of the year when we celebrate the coming of Christ that constantly reminds us of the power of His life to change things. He recalled that "Silent Night" was written because the organ was broken. He assured me that God is able to take the broken things to create magnificent music.

2. Project a spirit of optimism in spite of all the dark things that have happened. Remember: not all of your people have been involved in the division. The leader of a crisis church can become like the parents of a troubled teenager who focus only on the problem child and neglect the others. Refuse to let that happen at your church. Surround yourself with those who nourish you to compensate for those who sap your strength.

3. Attempt to minister to the main body of believers as a normal congregation. Concentrate your energies on the good things that are happening as you allow the Holy Spirit to work through your ministry. Refuse to allow the negative people to dominate your horizon.

4. Rest assured that if the patient dies in spite of all you have

attempted to do and everything falls apart, you haven't fallen apart. You are a valuable, highly regarded servant of God, and your outstanding pastoral record will speak for itself.

5. Keep on praying for the miracle you know God can provide. Does that guarantee instant answers? No, but many other wonderful things happen in a beleaguered servant and to his people when they pray. So keep up the prayer effort. In the flyleaf of Warren Wiersbe's copy of *The Disciplined Life*, V. Raymond Edman wrote, "Remember always to keep chin up and knees down!"[28]

6. Be assured that you are not out there alone, isolated and forgotten.

There are many who grieve with you and will continue to boldly approach the throne of God, believing that victory will come. Hang on and just continue to be the sensitive, caring, and victorious person you're known to be.

Remember—no matter how painful or disappointing your service may seem to you, it's not being wasted. Why not phone a friend who serves in a place where seldom is heard an encouraging word? Or send a letter or E-mail to a beleaguered colleague who's struggling to survive. Even if your own situation seems impossible, the act of encouraging someone else will certainly bolster you as well. "We can only keep on going, after all, by the power of God, who first saved us and then called us to this holy work" (2 Tim. 1:8-9, TM).

8　Ministry-Killers

*Your danger is not in being on the edge of a precipice,
but in being unwatchful there.*
—Author unknown

*Keep your heart with all vigilance,
for from it flow the springs of life.*
—Prov. 4:23, NRSV

As you've probably already realized, the journey of a comeback leader is not an easy one. I'm writing this in retrospect, much like a mountain climber after a long, hard climb. I'm looking back at the trail I've covered, and I can hardly believe that I made the journey to the top of the mountain. No, I haven't arrived. But I have the vantage point of experience, and the view is breathtaking. At times, the actual climb has tested every ounce of stamina I possess. And as one who has persevered, I have a final message that will either make you or break you. Realize as you read this chapter that one dangerous misjudgment in the areas specified can send you careening off a cliff to the death of your ministry.

There are definite, calculated risks in leading a comeback church. You face a difficult challenge, and while God's supernatural power will bring you success, there are also opportunities for failure. On the front lines you'll face unwelcome attacks on you and your family that you probably never counted on. These attacks, coupled with the stress of trying to reclaim what the evil one has conquered, can weaken you and cause you to fall in other areas. This chapter is devoted to addressing the key areas that can lead to the downfall of a mighty warrior of righteousness. It's paramount that you guard your life in many areas. These key areas include futile comparisons, stress overload, family strain, and marital infidelity.

Futile Comparisons

Every pastor is tempted to compare himself with others. I'm going to tell you about three kinds of fruitless comparisons: comparing yourself to pastors with easier assignments, comparing yourself to pastors who you think are more "successful," and comparisons made by others—perhaps your congregation—that are unfair and hurt you.

If you're presently in a difficult assignment, quit comparing yourself with other pastors you think have easier assignments than you do. In John 21:20, Peter saw John (the self-designated "disciple whom Jesus loved") eavesdropping on his conversation with Jesus after he had been told that his service would end in death. Peter asked, "What about him?" (v. 21) Perhaps Peter thought John was getting off easy or that more was asked of him than of John. The comparison game is fruitless and frustrating. Jesus clarified, "If I want him to remain alive until I return, what is that to you? *You* must follow me" (v. 22, emphasis added). There is no such thing as equality of demands. What God requires of me He may not require of you. The question is this: Will you pursue God's vision for *your* life? If so, get your eyes off others who seem to have an easier assignment. Focus on following Christ, even though at times the stress is unbearable.

Comparing yourself to the pastor you think is more successful is also an exercise in futility. Dwell there for long, and you'll wonder why you don't get the breaks other pastors have gotten. This self-deprecating behavior is demeaning and holds you down with feelings of worthlessness and failure to achieve. God may have you right where you need to be at this point in your development as a leader. It's one thing to want to achieve a larger assignment because you know you're capable, but it's quite another to feel unsuccessful because you haven't achieved what someone else has. Such comparisons lead to jealousy and are counterproductive. Avoid them at all cost.

Comparisons that others make of you are often subtle but no less tormenting. Perhaps you followed a very likeable pastor, and his or her strength is your weakness. If you begin to hear undue praise for your predecessor's strengths, you may be tempted to put yourself down because you never receive that kind of adulation. Recognize this for what it is—a compliment of their former pastor's strong points. Refuse to believe it is a putdown for your weaknesses. Otherwise, you'll make yourself miserable. Comparisons are futile for any reason. Accept yourself as God accepts you and your assignment as something He would entrust to none other.

Stress Overload

In 1 Kings 19, Elijah, one of the greatest prophets of the Bible, had just won the contest with the prophets of Baal on Mt. Carmel. The God who answered by fire (1 Kings 18:38) had proven himself true. Elijah had then seized the false prophets and slaughtered them with the sword. When Jezebel heard of this, she threatened to do the same to Elijah (19:1-2). Under normal circumstances a threat like that would have rolled off. But having come through the grueling experience on Mt. Carmel, his clothes still blood-splattered, Elijah tucked tail and ran. When you're up physically and emotionally, idle threats won't even faze you. But when you're battle-fatigued as Elijah was or have been through an extended period of over-stress, threats stick like a Velcro ball on a felt dartboard.

God chased after Elijah and found him collapsed under a tree so seriously depressed that he asked God to take his life—a prayer God seldom answers. Elijah was there because of overstress and exhaustion. A little stress is needed to help us grow spiritually and emotionally, but too much can kill. If we exceed our internal balance or quota of stress, what has been healthy stress that promotes growth turns to overstress and leads to burnout, depression, and disease.

Elijah's internal tachometer had redlined. The warning light on his dashboard had come on, trumpeting the message "Service engine." Drivers take that message seriously because something is obviously wrong with the engine. Similarly, pastors should pay attention to the physical manifestations of overstress. When Elijah's engine light came on, he coasted to a stop under the nearest tree. He put up his hood, sat down on the curb, and said, "I can't take any more." But when he went so far as to say, "I think I'd be better off dead," the Lord took notice and made a caring response.

Elijah was suffering from posttraumatic stress. He had just come through an extremely violent experience of carnage. He came to a stop under the most welcome bush of the desert. The juniper, or broom tree, always grew where there was ample water and shelter from the wind and sun. There God found Elijah and cared for his weary servant. God knew that what he needed most was rest, so first, He put him to sleep. God understands how physically, emotionally, and spiritually drained His servants can get. He didn't try to talk Elijah out of his negative feelings. He simply gave him a hot meal. The cake the Lord baked was so nutritious, so restoring, that he didn't need to eat again for 40 days. Some kind of energy bar! By the time God got through refreshing him with rest and food and more rest, Elijah was able to get up and go on.

Over the next 40 days, Elijah moved from the tree to a cave on Mount Horeb. Once again, the Lord went looking for Elijah, found him hiding in the darkness of a cave, and asked him, "What are you doing here?" Just because we survive one bout with serious depression is no guarantee we'll never be discouraged again. Something had gone wrong again, for Elijah made a wrong assessment: "I have been very zealous for the LORD God Almighty. The Israelites have rejected your covenant, broken down your altars, and put your prophets to death with the sword. I am the only one left, and now they are trying to kill me too" (19:10). He thought his efforts had been futile. God saw beyond his words and put on quite a show of power. But not one of these spectacular signs moved Elijah. What really assured him was the Lord's gentle whisper of assurance.

Elijah was gently corrected when he repeated his sad story of woe in verse 14. Verbalizing your grief to a caring person who is willing to listen helps a lot. What the Lord tried to do was get him out of the cave of discouragement. Just to entice him to the cave's entrance was not enough. God knew Elijah needed a whole new sense of direction. Almost as an aside, God said, "By the way, Elijah, you're wrong about being the only one left. I have 7,000 people just as zealous for me as you are!" In other words, Elijah was more successful than he had thought.

Steven L. Burns writes, "Carrying too heavy a stress load is like running your car engine past the red line; or leaving your toaster stuck in the 'on' position; or running a nuclear reactor past maximum permissible power. Sooner or later, something will break, burn up, or melt down. What breaks depends on where the weak links are in your physical body."[1] Your brain, gastrointestinal tract, glandular system, cardiovascular, skin, and immune system all bear the brunt of overstress. Fatigue, aches and pains, crying spells, depression, anxiety attacks, sleep disturbance, ulcers, cramps and diarrhea, colitis, irritable bowel, thyroid gland malfunction, high blood pressure, heart attack, abnormal heart beat, stroke, itchy skin rashes, and decreased resistance to infections may all be traced to the physical damage of overstress.

My first comeback church experience came in my mid-20s when I was inexperienced and far less mature than I thought I was when I strutted confidently across the platform to receive my seminary diploma. I was ready to take on the world, but when I went into the ministry and was unable to control outcomes or people, I internalized much of the stress. Our church bus was repossessed after the donor refused to pay the bill. With never enough money to balance the budget, financial concerns took a toll. I began to wake up in the middle of the night with severe chest pains. It got so bad that I couldn't bear the weight of my body against the mattress. For six weeks, each night I stayed in the bed until awakened by excruciating pain and then slept the rest of the night sitting in a recliner.

I sought medical help, but nothing definitive was diagnosed. Heart problems were quickly ruled out, but the pain continued. I took muscle-relaxers and painkillers. My doctor thought I might have a viral infection, so I received large antibiotic injections every other day for several weeks. A short stay in the hospital for extensive tests brought the diagnosis of costochondritis—inflammation of the nerve endings that line the chest wall. There may have been physical reasons for this condition, but when the doctor asked me about the stress level in my life, I knew he suspected overstress. The pain eventually subsided through treatment with a regimen of steroids. I had to learn better ways of coping with the stress of ministry, or my health was going to break before I reached 30.

My first comeback church took a toll, although we had successfully doubled the attendance in two years. I had so much yet to learn. I grew restless and opted for a youth pastor position under a seasoned senior pastor until I was ready to try another comeback church challenge. I matured a lot in that brief two-year respite, so much so that I survived my second comeback church experience without immediate physical complications.

However, the physical effects of my second comeback experience did show up when I was heavily involved in the task of following a forced-out pastor in my third assignment. The cumulative effects of prolonged overstress landed me in the hospital with unexplainable back pain. No physical reason other than overstress could be found for my symptoms. I began to overeat. One day in my mid-30s I looked at myself in the mirror and didn't like what I saw. I was 20 pounds overweight, rapidly developing a double chin, and feeling horrible. I called myself to accountability and began a diet in an attempt to fight back.

As a matter of self-discipline, I avoided diet pills and began to deny myself certain fatty foods in an attempt to change my eating habits. I lost 25 pounds in about three months, but as soon as I went off the diet, the weight came back. This was when I literally started running for my life. I gradually worked up to five miles at least three times a week. Did I say how much I like to eat? I discovered that if I maintained the running discipline, I could eat heartily. What a deal! Running has another benefit: stress relief. I could not nurse my hurts or even rehearse them while running. To survive the stress of a comeback effort, walk, jog, or work out. You must establish an ongoing regimen of exercise for your physical and mental well-being.

Also realize what I finally learned: *two in a row and out you go.* In other words, if you endure two gut-wrenching experiences of unbearable stress without giving yourself time for rest and renewal, then the light on your dashboard will start flashing, "Service engine." These experiences can come in the form of ministry demands, people problems, or member losses outside your control. Two tough assignments in succession without a time for healing and replenishment, and you may be tempted to leave the ministry.

Comeback pastors are not exempt from the whirling rush of life and ministry. Even those who lead seemingly healthy lives can become overwhelmed. When stress exceeds your ability to cope, the result is emotional and physical illness. Overstress plays no favorites. Rich or poor, young or old, prophet or pastors—all are potential targets for overload.

Survival Strategies for Stress

1. **Pay attention to the warning signs of overstress.** Stop and rest or seek the help you need in order to be refreshed. Take some time off, and let God restore you physically and mentally. Remember: without proper stress recuperation, two in a row and out you go.

2. **Develop a consistent exercise routine.** Aside from being healthy, exercise relieves stress and increases energy. It will make you feel younger and increase your physical stamina.

3. **Realize that you're not alone.** With fresh assurance that he was not alone, Elijah was told to go back the way he came, to face the things he had been running from, and to realize that he was not alone in his assignment. Elijah was reminded that the Lord is always with His prophets, forever holding them up.

4. **Give up your feelings of failure.** God is always doing more than may appear above the surface. He will provide a way out or a way through. If you've lost your zeal to keep going, if you're tired and drained, if the whirling rush of ministry has thrown you off balance, your perspective is skewed.

5. **Overstress leads to under-assessment.** You're in no position to judge your effectiveness or success when you're overstressed. Seek rest and renewal. Do your best, and leave the results to God.

Family Strain

I went to seminary single in what at the time was a married man's institution. I worked a full-time job loading freight at a truck line in addition to carrying a full academic load. I met my wife the week after Christmas vacation. I had been laid off from my job, so I bought a plane ticket to go home to Miami. I specifically remember praying during the holidays that God would lead me to the person He had for me to marry. Incredibly, the woman who became my wife got saved (after rebelling against God for several years) the very week I was praying for a wife. We met my first Sunday back in school after Christmas and were married eight months later.

Kaye would tell you that she didn't realize what she was getting into.

She had once said, "I'll never marry a preacher or a redhead!" She ate those words when she married me. Through the years, she has eaten plenty of other words as well, some related to our various assignments. The extreme pressure of taking comeback assignments affected our home and family. Like Kaye, most pastors' wives assume the role by virtue of their love for their husbands. Most wives don't fully comprehend the cost.

How can we reduce the stress of a comeback effort on our wives and families? The following are four lessons I learned the hard way through trial and error.

1. Avoid spillover stress.

Try as we may to shield our wives and families from the unplanned pressures, there's considerable spillover. If you're not careful, you can unwittingly make those dearest to you the brunt of your pressure and frustration. I could have been a better lover, a better demonstrator of love, a better expresser of love to assure Kaye—to uplift her. But at times overstress made me far too self-absorbed. I wish I had put as much energy into enriching my marriage as I put into complaining. I've learned to affirm my spouse five times as much as I criticize her.

My pastor dad wrote me a letter during my second comeback experience and pleaded with me to do better than he thought he had done while raising his family. "Looking back," he confessed, "I was too enclosed with myself—with a consuming passion to succeed and took myself too seriously. Thus the frustrations scored hard against my stomach, my disposition, my sense of mission and joy." With incredible honesty he revealed, "I too often took it out on Mom and the kids—the ones I dearly loved the best of all." Fortunately, childhood memories are void of what Dad confessed.

His letter continued, "The extent to which frustrations, setbacks, and so forth got to me, I became less effective, (a) as lover of my wife; and (b) comprehending and acknowledging the personhood of my children." He told me that I should call this "advice" or "remorse" or whatever I deemed necessary. I see now that my preacher dad wanted to be sure that I didn't make the mistakes that he felt he had made.

2. Watch your words.

It's very easy to hurt the ones we love. Our loved ones deserve more than the anger and frustration we feel in the midst of crisis. Even if you grew up in a staid, unexpressive home where seldom was heard an encouraging word, you can break out of that. Care must be taken to use affectionate words like "Honey" and "Sweetheart" and "I love you" when you're in a difficult situation. Remember, as Robert Schuller has said, that our words can be "bullets, bombs, or blessings." In the throes of a comeback church experience, we made a conscious effort not to take our frustrations out on each other or the kids, but at times we failed miserably.

3. Make your home a safe haven.

In *Leadership*, Joe McKeever said he and his wife, Margaret, designated their porch at home as the place where they would talk about church. "There," he said, "we would discuss any nasty thing anybody said or did, but we refused to bring it into the house."[2] Your home must be a safe haven for your children. Extreme caution must be taken in the presence of your children to shield their minds and hearts from being poisoned by the negative experiences of church life. The McKeevers were on to something. They understood that pressures would come and planned on a way to vent them that prevented negativism from infecting their home. Lanson Ross taught this principle in a seminar at our fourth comeback church when he said, "Pressure isn't pressure when it's planned pressure. Pre-determining your difficult times and planning around them" can reduce overstress. Decide in advance how you'll respond when problems show up, as they surely will. This helps take the pressure off.

4. Divorce is not a viable option.

Ministry in the throes of a comeback experience can be hazardous to your marriage and family. Your relationship with your spouse will be either strengthened or strained. In our second comeback effort, the daily onslaught of crisis and extreme pressure led us to consider divorce. When you seek relief, no option is excluded. Kaye struggled between loyalty to her children and loyalty to my calling as a comeback pastor. She desperately wanted to get our children out of the mess that was spilling over into our family life. Only prayer and commitment to each other kept us from seeing our marriage crash on the rocks. In the end, divorce was unthinkable to both of us. Not only did we love each other deeply, but divorce also would have ended our ministry. We decided that since we were going to stay married, we would give ourselves the gift of a good marriage.

At times the despair became crippling, leaving us incapable of functioning effectively at even the most mundane tasks. Things happened that stung, hurt, and brought tears. The incessant emotional overload took its toll. I developed deep creases in my forehead and dark bags under my eyes. These things were just a part of the cost of the comeback effort.

Survival Strategies for Marital Strain

1. Show your kids a special love relationship.

Your relationship to your spouse is primary. In *Raising Responsible Kids*, Jay Kessler suggests that you must "love your spouse more than your kids."[3] I agree, as long as in doing this your children don't need to feel that it's a "them against us" setup. I've seen couples who make certain their kids know that the marriage is first and in doing so alienate their kids. I had a mother tell me that she loves her husband supremely but would never tell her children, "We love each other more than we love you" or "Our marriage relationship is more important." Such words may wound children for life and make them feel alienated in their own homes, or at least will communicate to them that they're only second rate.

Recently this woman's daughter said, "Dad, do you love me or Mom most?" And they agreed in front of her that they had a different love for her than for each other but that they loved her completely. What kids need is the security of unconditional love, not to be injured by feelings of competition for their parents' love and affection. Down deep inside all of us, we all need unconditional love. That includes children. And even though that young mother said she loves her husband even more than her own children, she'll never put them in an emotional situation in which they feel as if they're pitted against their own father for her love. One day when they're adults and are gone, they'll understand and will say, "Mom and Dad have something really special." But for now, they can't understand because they're too young. All your children need is to feel completely loved. That's why I say to show them the special love relationship you have.

This is important for comeback pastors with young children, because the upheaval from church can and will affect the family. The last thing a pastor needs is for his or her children to feel less loved. But also, protect and nurture your relationship with each other, loving your spouse supremely above home, furniture, car, baby, career, or anything that might come between you. Charles L. Allen in *God's Psychiatry* said, "For a happy marriage, a lot of things are not necessary. Money and the things money can buy are good to have but can be done without. Two things in marriage that must exist: (1) a solid affection, a love for each other entirely different from the love for anyone else; and (2) complete trust in each other."[4]

2. Keep the courtship going.

Tenaciously protect the urges and attractions that brought you together in the first place. Prioritize marriage in your schedule. Write love notes and letters. Invest time, effort, and money on a date day or date night. One memorable Christmas, Kaye gave me a colorful metal box wrapped in a Christmas bow. Inside were 52 notes individually tied with a smaller bow. Her idea was for me to open one each week. The notes were gifts, entitlements, or pleasures that put a spark in our relationship. On our 32nd anniversary we were heavily engaged in the opening service of a denominational assembly, but not so busy that I couldn't stop in the middle of the service and present her with a dozen roses and a public kiss.

3. Be a servant leader at home.

Many spouses might as well have signs around their necks that say, "What I do best is serve!" Try turning the tables at home by cooking, cleaning, or serving your spouse. After your spouse awakens from fainting, he or she really will appreciate being served.

4. Affirm and encourage your mate.

Give your mate the freedom to be the person God made him or her to be. Avoid criticism and putdowns like the plague. Put as much energy into enriching your marriage as you do into complaining. Never belittle, manipulate, or intentionally discourage your mate. Look for the good and point that out, always seeking new ways to build up your spouse. Come out and say it. Express your love verbally and in writing.

5. Pull in the same direction.

There may be times when you don't pull in the same direction. But then you must stop and remove the obstacles so you can. Like two locomotives hitched to the same train but going in opposite directions, there's nothing but sparks and smoke. When both spouses pull in the same direction, the heaviest loads can be pulled together. If your mate is going in the opposite direction from where you're going, your ministry can't be effective. Regrettably, some have had to leave pastoral ministry in order to save their marriages. Others seek an alternative ministry role that requires less of their spouses—because, as the old saying goes, "When Mama ain't happy, ain't nobody happy!" Happiness comes when we're joyfully yoked—even in a difficult assignment—because we know we're right where God wants us to be.

6. Keep your communication open and honest.

Talk to each other. Care enough to confront even if you must traverse for a time through the "tunnel of chaos." If you never discuss misunderstandings, reveal hurt feelings, air frustrations, or ask difficult questions, your relationship will deteriorate, and feelings of love will be replaced with detachment, distrust, and bitterness. Deal daily with any unfinished business even though for a time the verbal tunnel seems frightening. Bill Hybels says that when you come out the other side, "you will find that the tunnel was a small price to pay for the open communication and freed-up love of an authentic relationship."[5]

7. Try a lot of tenderness.

Hug. Convey love through touch affirmingly, sensually, and unpredictably. Show small acts of kindness. Commit yourself to sexual fidelity. Meet your spouse's sexual needs. Strive for intimacy spiritually, physically, and emotionally. Learn the language of love. Never seek to satisfy your sexual desires elsewhere.

8. Apologize sincerely and forgive.

Accept the fact that you'll make mistakes and that perfection is not a worthy goal. End each day with a clean slate. Keep no record of wrongs.

9. Focus on the fun side.

Spend time with your mate for no other reason than to have a good time. Learn to have fun together developing some common fun interests: golf, jogging, walking, or going to garage sales. You name it. Break up the routine, and the spark in your relationship can be reignited.

10. Check the gauges on the dashboard of your life.

Work at prevention before you have a crisis. Saying you don't have a problem doesn't work. That's denial. "Denial ain't just a river in Egypt." Check your spiritual pulse regularly.

Marital Infidelity

To celebrate our 25th anniversary, my wife and I took the dream trip of a lifetime to the island of Maui for two wonderful weeks of golf, beachcombing, snorkel diving, whale watching, and sightseeing. Friends told us that we should drive the road to Hana to see the volcano at sunrise. To have any hope of viewing the expansive crater, we needed to be on the road by 2:30 A.M. That was a bit early for us, but we decided to make the drive anyway. Sure enough, by 9:00 the clouds and rain had already obscured the sun.

The road to Hana is a sport car enthusiast's dream, presenting a challenging series of hairpin curves. I came to appreciate the presence of guardrails. The higher we climbed on the winding road, the more spectacular the view was. I could hardly bear to look, knowing the drop was several thousand feet in some places. Fear kept my hands glued to the steering wheel as we wound our way through the mountainous terrain.

Guardrails exist in dangerous places to protect drivers from certain death. If the brakes fail or the car goes out of control, the guardrails keep the car's occupants safe from disaster. Only fools purposely see how close to the edge they can get or disregard guardrails. Guardrails are for emergencies. You cannot hit a guardrail or even scrape against one without damage to your vehicle. Scraping or swiping a guardrail requires a trip to the body shop.

If a comeback pastor is to survive morally on the curves of the moral road to Hana, attention must be paid to the guardrails of godliness. These are posted at the edge, the point beyond which you cannot go without irreparable harm. Only fools intentionally brush against these soul safeguards. On the road to Hana, we were in a rental car that belonged to someone else. We assumed liability for any damage that might be done to their vehicle. The same is true of our bodies. These vessels belong to God because He paid for them (see 1 Cor. 7:23). Our bodies are on loan from God as the temple of the Holy Spirit (see 6:19). Therefore, we must honor God with our bodies and do no harm against God's property, bought and paid for by Christ himself (see v. 20).

Sexual temptation is the area most ministers are held least accountable and where they can fall fastest. None is exempt, so how can we protect ourselves, our families, and Christ's Church from the devastating effects of a moral lapse? Intercession is vital, but so are some boundaries beyond which we refuse to go.

Ministers are not alone. Research indicates that non-Christian and Christian men are falling into sexual sin in unprecedented numbers. As many as 40 to 45 percent of all married men have extramarital affairs. For men under age 40, the figure rises to 70 percent. In *Guard Your Heart*, Gary Rosberg speaks to every man:

> It's no coincidence that many men fall in this area. But falling into sexual sin is rarely a fluke. Healthy relationships and healthy choices don't just "go bad" all at once. Relationships don't collapse—they *erode*. Adultery doesn't just happen. Men don't suddenly walk away from a marriage commitment like an ox to the slaughter. Adultery doesn't begin in the perfumed darkness of a hotel room nor with little flirtations in the office hallway. Adultery begins in the heart with a single thought in an unguarded moment. The momentum builds from there.[6]

When one minister falls, we all fall. According to C. Peter Wagner, "If a pastor falls, more people are hurt and set back in their spiritual lives than if others fall. The ripple effect is incredibly devastating."[7] This is not a place for smug self-sufficiency nor irrational boasting that such a thing will never happen to me; rather, it's a time to take heed lest *we* fall (see 1

Cor. 10:12). Hence, there is a need to make sure some safeguards are always in place.

As a comeback church pastor, you'll be targeted for spiritual warfare. Believers are the targets, but pastors and their families have bull's-eyes painted on their backs. Why? Because Satan hates comeback churches that have been resurrected from the dead and have sprung forth to vitality. Such churches bring glory and honor and praise to Jesus. If Satan can divert glory from Christ and His kingdom, he will use any means or method, including but not limited to the destruction of pastors and their families.

Leaders are just as subject to temptation as anyone else, perhaps more so. As Wagner cautions, "The higher up you go on the ladder of Christian leadership, the higher you go on Satan's hit list."[8] In a statement credited to Howard Hendricks, H. B. London reminds us that "Satan will lie in the weeds for 40 years to entrap one of God's servants."[9] Satan is patient, he will wait, and he will watch for just the right moment—a moment that will do the greatest damage to the kingdom of God. As the editors of *Leadership* concluded, "If you think you can't fall into sexual sin, then you're godlier than David, stronger than Samson, and wiser than Solomon."[10]

The integrity crisis continues. Back in 1988, Warren Wiersbe made a telling admission in his book entitled *The Integrity Crisis*. "Both the ministry and the message of the church have lost credibility before a watching world, and the world seems to be enjoying the spectacle. 'Why should we listen to the church?' the critical world is asking. 'By what authority do you Christians preach to us about sin and salvation?' Set your own house in order, and then we may want to listen to you."[11] The truth is, leaders are human and just as subject to the devil's schemes as anyone else; but try to tell that to a watching world that puts ministers on a pedestal.

It's not a sin to be tempted, and we can't avoid temptation altogether. We can, however, avoid recklessly slamming into the guardrails. Disregarding them or exploring on the other side of them is sure disaster. Those who fall disregard the guardrails of godliness. Take heed of the words of C. S. Lewis: "Think of me as a fellow-patient in the same hospital who, having been admitted a little earlier, could give some advice."[12]

1. Guardrail no. 1: A strong relationship with God.

Attention must be paid to the care of your soul on a daily basis. An unguarded heart is a vulnerable one. If you don't develop intimacy with God by giving yourself fully to the Lord, you're basically saying that you can pretty much handle whatever comes your way in your own strength. One fallen minister admitted that his first step to moral decline involved pulling away from his core relationship with the Lord. In the place of a powerful spiritual existence grew a system of talking a truth he wasn't living. We can never fall into the trap of saying the words without the reality in our hearts. A trilogy for failure in ministry is *overwork, overtired, under-prayed.*

2. Guardrail no. 2: Extreme caution with the opposite sex.

We must set strict boundaries for ourselves. Build a high hedge without closing yourself off from people. Restrict your compliments of the opposite sex to character issues.

Authors Stanley J. Grentz and Roy D. Bell in a *Leadership* article entitled "Predator, Wanderer, or Lover" state that taking precaution means being alert to the signs that a relationship is approaching the forbidden zone. However, violation of the boundaries of proper intimacy rarely occurs imperceptibly. Generally, moral failure begins with a thousand little letdowns.[13]

3. Guardrail no. 3: A wide-open relationship with a same-gender accountability partner.

A same-gender accountability partner must be a person with whom you can honestly share your struggles and areas of weakness. Good friends can keep their antennas up to see if we're drifting into dangerous territory with members of the opposite sex. We do need each other, and we can encourage and strengthen each other in deeply significant ways. We must find someone who will look us in the eye and ask us if we've kept ourselves pure.

4. Guardrail no. 4: A satisfying relationship with your spouse.

"Your spring water is for you and you only, not to be passed around among strangers. Bless your fresh-flowing fountain! Enjoy the wife you married as a young man! Lovely as an angel, beautiful as a rose—don't ever quit taking delight in her body. Never take her love for granted! Why would you trade enduring intimacies for cheap thrills with a whore? For dalliance with a promiscuous stranger?" (Prov. 5:15-19, TM). If you're sexually thirsty, head for your own well—the well God has provided for you. Quench your thirst at your own fountain instead of roaming around looking for another. Don't say no to each other too often. Since I can hardly imagine a man saying no, perhaps this caution is aimed at those women who are not sympathetic to their man's needs in this area and say no too often. I believe that in many—maybe almost all—cases when a man, especially a minister falls, his wife continually turns a cold shoulder.

Debra White Smith deals honestly and directly with these issues with women in *Romancing Your Husband*. I heartily recommend this book, because it could help save marriages. Debra's concern is that some wives actually shove their husbands right into the guardrails by their selfishness and lack of concern for their husbands' needs.

In Gary Rosberg's words, "You don't need other women or images of other women to soothe your soul. The woman you met at the end of the wedding aisle would walk across America to receive you if you took a shot at building intimacy in your marriage. In two words: It works. In two more words: Try it."[14] Don't allow your marriage to become marred by mediocrity. Don't settle for just getting by.

Overstress can kill you physically and mentally. Unbearable stress can also have a negative impact on your marriage and family. But to survive morally and avoid actual or virtual infidelity, we must put some guardrails in place or become a casualty on the mountainous cliffs of Temptation Island.

Survival Strategies for Sexual Temptation

1. When with the opposite sex, avoid conversation of an increasingly personal or sexual nature.

The details of sexual problems with the opposite sex should not be discussed in counseling. If you fail to understand the reality of transference in counseling, you won't know when the counselee's marital or sexual problems become your own needs and problems.

2. Exercise extreme caution in expressing affection to your parishioners.

Questionable physical contacts through friendly pats, hugging, even "butterfly kisses" are subject to misinterpretation. Thank God for His grace for some of the close calls and seemingly innocent acts that could have destroyed your ministry.

3. Discipline your thought life.

If you begin to fantasize about a sexual relationship with a parishioner, you have already mentally crossed the line. My mother used to give some homespun advice by quoting a familiar saying: "You can't keep the birds from flying over your head, but you can keep them from making a nest in your hair!" Remember: you're not what you think; rather, what you think, you are.

4. Watch what you're watching.

Destruction is a mouse click away. What starts out as curiosity can quickly lead to downfall. You may never visit an adult bookstore, but pornography is only a mouse click away via the Internet. The anonymous nature of the Internet has broken down the traditional barriers to pornography and offers new channels leading to more sexual addictions and problems. In a Focus on the Family article announcing a new ministry called "Pure Intimacy," a Zogby survey indicates that one in five self-proclaimed born-again Christians have visited sexually oriented web sites. A *Leadership* survey suggested that four in ten pastors have visited a pornographic web site. And more than one-third have done so in the past year.[15]

One anonymous pastor revealed that he turned on the computer and then the computer turned on him. He had stumbled onto a pornographic site accidentally. At first he turned off his computer, but he confessed that later he went back several times, feeling guilty each time. This "straight-arrow pastor" became hooked and began visiting unspeakable sites on his office computer. He did so at home until his wife discovered that "someone had been looking at Internet porn on our computer." He denied doing so, accusing one of the kids, so she dropped the matter. Thereafter, he confined his voyeurism to the church office computer, obsessively masturbating in the church restroom. While he never would have visited his town's red-light district or the local porn shop, all this and more were available electronically. Once addicted, this pastor often switched between his Bible software and hardcore porn sites, spending hours each week staring at the screen. His "virtual infidelity" eventually led to a momentary indiscretion with a parishioner. Eventually the pastor confessed to his wife and district superintendent his sordid addiction, resulting in discipline and a loss of his ministry.[16] Pornography must be avoided at all costs. So watch what you're watching. Never turn down that road. But if you have, turn back and seek professional help.

5. Avoid meeting alone with a parishioner of the opposite sex.

Even over lunch in a public place or outside a customary office setting, don't meet alone with a parishioner of the opposite sex. Don't offer to drive a member of the opposite sex home alone. Agree to meet or counsel a parishioner of the opposite sex only if accompanied by your spouse or some other third party. Another protection is to have doors with windows installed in your office. Make your secretary and spouse your protective allies.

6. If you have to lie to your spouse about an action, don't do it.

If you felt "funny" about a gesture or a remark that made you uncomfortable, share that with your spouse. My wife has a great antenna and can alert me of women I especially need to be careful around. Kaye seems to have a sense of when a woman's actions around me seem overly flirtatious. It has happened frequently. Frankly, if anybody ever made a pass at Kaye or me, we would both just faint! I do remember a few occasions when she said after observing my overly flirtatious response, "That's one you better watch out for." Or if she saw me making an idiot of myself, she would call my attention to the fact that I was making myself look foolish. Your spouse should be your ally in protection. James

Dobson talks about two ways to have a flat tire: a blowout or a slow leak. "In marriage," he says, "if one partner becomes a drifter, the other must act like a parent and pull him or her back."[17]

Maybe instead of praying for a way *out*, your prayer should be to find a way *through*. The Christian life was never intended to be a life of escape from adversity but rather a conquest over it. Christians in general, and comeback pastors in particular, must learn to persevere. Bolster your faith with the humble avowal that you can do all things through Christ, who gives the strength (Phil. 4:13). You can control the comparisons you make, although you may be unable to control the comparisons others make of you. Pay attention to the signs of overstress, and practice preventative measures to reduce the behaviors that lead to dangerous burnout. Put some guardrails in place to protect yourself against sexual temptation, and your ministry can survive the most difficult comeback assignment.

9 Bridge-Builders

The task ahead of us is never as great as the power behind us.
                                                    —Author unknown

*Now it's up to you. Be on your toes—both for yourselves and your
congregation of sheep. The Holy Spirit has put you in charge of
these people—God's people they are—to guard and protect them.
God himself thought they were worth dying for.*
                                                    —Acts 20:28, TM

I would like to share a story that's a parable on the task of the
comeback church pastor. I've seen myself in this story and shared it on a
return trip to one of my former comeback churches for an anniversary
celebration.

Once upon a time, two brothers who lived on adjoining farms fell
into conflict. It was the first serious rift in 40 years of farming side by
side, sharing machinery, and trading labor and goods as needed without
a hitch. Then the long collaboration fell apart. It began with a small misunderstanding, grew into a major difference, and finally exploded into
an exchange of bitter words followed by weeks of silence.

One morning there was a knock on John's door. He opened it to find
a man with a carpenter's toolbox. "I'm looking for a few days' work," he
said. "Perhaps you would have a few small jobs here and there. Could I
help you?"

"Yes," said the older brother. "I do have a job for you. Look across
the creek at that farm. That's my neighbor; in fact, it's my younger brother. Last week there was a meadow between us. He took his bulldozer to
the river levee, and now it's a creek between us.

"Well, he may have done this to spite me, but I'll go him one better.
See that pile of lumber curing by the barn? I want you to build a fence—
an eight-foot fence—so I won't need to see his place anymore. Cool him
down anyhow."

The carpenter said, "I think I understand the situation. Show me the nails and the posthole digger, and I'll be able to do a job that pleases you."

The older brother had to go to town for supplies, so he helped the carpenter get the materials ready, and then he was off for the day. The carpenter worked hard all that day measuring, sawing, and nailing.

About sunset when the farmer returned, his eyes opened wide and his jaw dropped. There was no fence there at all! It was a bridge—a bridge stretching from one side of the creek to the other. A fine piece of work—handrails and all—and the neighbor, his younger brother, was coming across, his hand outstretched.

"You're quite a fellow to build this bridge after all I've said and done."

The two brothers stood at each end of the bridge and then met in the middle, taking each other's hand. They turned to see the carpenter hoist his toolbox on his shoulder.

"No, wait! Stay a few days. I have a lot of other projects for you," said the older brother.

"I'd love to stay on," the carpenter said, "but I have many more bridges to build."

Bridges of Reconciliation Needed

As we work through the first few years of this new millennium, we have many bridges yet to build. With 193 denominations and more than 350,000 churches in the United States alone, the likelihood is that the church you serve right now may have a river running through it. A bridge is needed, and the task of building it is yours. Some may think your assignment is to build a fence. There are two sides to a comeback experience: the catastrophe (what caused the decline of the church) and also the comeback (what led to the recovery). You're the carpenter. Take up your tools to become a bridge-builder. If Satan has cut a hole in the levee of unity your congregation once enjoyed, a creek now alienates brothers and sisters from each other. Build a bridge. Those on either side will extend their hands and meet in the middle if you courageously build the bridge.

The following ten suggestions will enable and equip you in your bridge-building endeavors. As you read them, begin now to listen for the voice of Jesus, the divine Carpenter. He will instruct you in exactly how to begin building the necessary bridges. Listen to Him. Trust Him. Know that He will be with you. Understand that His desires for your church's comeback exceed even your own. And with Him by your side, you will indeed witness a miracle.

1. Seek to discover God's plan.

Each comeback endeavor will require a unique set of blueprints that only God himself knows, and if the pastor is listening, he or she will get the exact instructions needed for the exact steps to take. Never forget that you have been sent to a church in need by the divine Carpenter to initiate His divine plan, not your own clever ideas. At my first comeback assignment—the church "looking up to see bottom" in a declining community—God's plan seemed to revolve around changing the inward focus to an outward one. At that church God led us to start a bus ministry that brought in children and their parents.

In our second comeback effort, a church severely divided doctrinally, God's plan was for me to seek a place where the congregation could stand together in unity. In comeback challenge number three, God's plan centered around drawing people back together after the forced termination of my predecessor. Comeback church four found itself submerged in a community where people were defecting because of economic recession. God's plan there was to focus on stabilizing issues, caring and sharing for people in need, and giving hope to the hopeless. My fifth comeback task was to a comfortable, middle class congregation that had been on a plateau for a decade. God's plan for this strong, but sleeping giant was to awaken it with a compelling vision for evangelism and ministry. And, finally, God's plan for my last comeback church, a severely fractured congregation, involved calling the church to prayer, resolving conflict according to biblical principles, and laying the groundwork for healing so that the church could move forward on its knees. As you can see, each comeback effort required the discovery of God's plan. However long it takes, seek His plan in your assignment. God has put that dissatisfaction with the way things are within you because He wants to use you to change them. God is able to turn a curse into a blessing (see Neh. 13:2).

2. Make a proper assessment.

There are no prefabricated blueprints for success. No matter how hard a pastor tries to build the bridge, it will fall through without the divine Carpenter telling him or her exactly what lumber to use and what nails to use, and so on. To paraphrase Ps. 127:1, "Unless the Lord builds the bridge, its builders labor in vain." Like the carpenter in the story, you'll have to take some time to listen and assess the problem. The older brother thought he needed a fence. The carpenter said, "I think I understand the situation," and proceeded to build a bridge instead. What your people may think they need may not be what God knows they need. For instance, at one of my assignments, the church board members who interviewed me said they wanted a healer. What they really meant was a deliverer to bring them out of bondage. Actually, they didn't know what they needed. What they really wanted was an end to the crisis.

The creek in the story seems quite small, small enough that a bridge could be built in a day. But creeks have a way of turning into flash floods when the rains come. So the size of bridge depends on the distance to be spanned. God has gifted you with the ability to size up what could be potential disaster and do what's necessary to keep a church from the brink of extinction. Don't allow fear of failure, people, finances, criticism from your colleagues, or even opposition to keep you from your appointed task.

3. Be sensitive to the past, but focus on the future.

In the story the creek remained. The breach in the river levee was not patched. A bridge was built over the effects of the break. The aftereffects of decline may remain. We don't know what the terrain looked like or felt like before the levee was intentionally ruptured, but that doesn't matter. Present reality includes past history. If the death of the church has been averted, stabilization at a much smaller size may be inevitable. But as George Barna reminds, "Because churches are nonprofit entities whose existence requires only a name and a person or two to maintain the legacy, a dead church is not necessarily an ex-church."[1]

If you pastor a church that's half the size it was during its "glory" days, I'm sure your people expect you to lead them back to greatness. Some think that once the Band-Aids come off, the church is well and should be growing again. You'll have your fill of people who describe the best of the past. But your job is the future. You operate in real time, and God will help you forge a new future. After major decline because of serious division, a decade or more may elapse before lost ground is reclaimed. Your people may *want* a quick fix, but there really is none.

I wonder if those two brothers ever considered rebuilding the levee and seeking to go back to the way things once had been. Perhaps too much water had gone under the bridge, so they had to make the best of their present realities. One of my favorite John Maxwell quotes came from a teaching session of the K-Church Project: "Although you cannot go back and make a brand-new start, you can start today and make a brand-new end." God is the God of another chance. You'll wonder at times if a church can get so far off track that it can never get back on again. But our confidence is that of the prophet Samuel: "For the sake of his great name the LORD will not reject his people, because the LORD was pleased to make you his own" (1 Sam. 12:22).

4. Take risks to do what's needed.

Comeback church leaders take calculated risks, doing what's necessary and not always what's popular. The carpenter did "a fine piece of work—handrails and all." He was hired to build a fence but built a bridge, because he considered the plausible outcomes of each and pursued the one that provided the greatest potential for success. The problem called for a bridge, so the carpenter took a risk even though he had been hired to build a fence. "Making the decision to accept a significant challenge—a challenge that might result in failure—is one of the most difficult aspects of the Christian pilgrimage." But as Scott Walker writes in *Life-Rails*, "The willingness to take risks in life is often the only difference between success and failure."[2] Commit your cause to God, and leave the results to Him.

When he saw the bridge, the younger brother assumed that his older brother had hired the carpenter to build it and responded with gestures of reconciliation. He came across, "his hand outstretched." The carpenter knew that two wrongs would not make a right. A fence for a creek would have been a monument to the failure of a relationship. But a bridge for a creek made reconciliation possible.

Your eyes must be open to see others' needs, both spiritual and material; your heart must be ready to care for needy souls when you find them; your mind must be alert to plan out the best way to help them; and your will must be set against the trick we are all so good at—passing the buck, going by on the other side, and contracting out of situations of need where sacrificial help is called for.[3]

The buck stops with you. No one except God himself can tell you what needs to be done in your situation. Friends and colleagues may try to tell you what to do, but you're the one on the front lines. Listen to advice, but consent to do only what the divine Carpenter tells you to do. If you become an expediter of the people's wants—a resource for their use—the people aren't being led but serviced. As Winston Churchill said, "It is not enough that we do our best; sometimes we have to do what's required."[4] You are in the best position to know what is required. You are uniquely qualified to accomplish God's plan. He has put you where you are for a purpose.

A cardinal rule of delegation states that he who is asked to do the job plans how it will be done.[5] A cardinal rule of the comeback effort should be that the comeback pastor gets to plan what approach should be taken. As long as you're taking your cues from the divine Carpenter, build a bridge even when others think you need a fence. He is into good outcomes. Garry Wills in *Certain Trumpets* reminds that "we have long lists of the leader's requisites—determination, focus, a clear goal, a sense of priorities, and so on. We easily forget the first and all-encompassing need—the leader most needs followers."[6] The acid test of leadership: is anybody following? So take a look over your shoulder and check to see whether anyone is following. God's blueprints are designed to bring His people along. If they aren't following, you might want to double-check the directions. "One-legged and two-legged chairs do not, of themselves, stand. A third leg is needed. Leader, followers, and goals make up the necessary supports for leadership."[7]

5. Take no credit for a spiritual success.

The selfless carpenter didn't correct the younger brother when he said, "You're quite a fellow to build this bridge after all I've said and done." He took no credit for the comeback in the brothers' relationship. It was not his idea. There's no mention of the carpenter's response when he saw the brothers meet "in the middle." Nothing of "I did that, you know," on the carpenter's part. He simply hoisted his toolbox onto his shoulder and prepared to move on, revealing his own spiritual depth.

The focus of the comeback effort is always Jesus Christ. The only success we can know is in relationship to Him. Always divert the glory to Christ in any comeback accomplishment. You'll be amazed at what you can accomplish if you don't care about who gets the credit. You may have to go through a period of brokenness. Alan E. Nelson puts it this way: "Brokenness seems to be a prerequisite that God demands before doing lasting work through a person."[8] Nelson has unearthed the key to lasting success—brokenness—"letting God take over your PR (public relations) department. Let God do your PR. Let God blow your whistle. God will advance you, in His way. He's got your address when it's time for the promotion."[9]

I'm convinced that I came to that experience of brokenness while at my last comeback assignment. I now see that the 11 months of accelerated prayer were to break me in the "right place," as Nelson describes. Pride pollutes your accomplishments. Humility promotes spiritual life, potential, perspective, and your future. The sooner we humble ourselves and refuse to take any credit or attention, the sooner the new assignment God has for us will come.

6. Stay until the task is completed.

Building the bridge may take a short time or a long time. My shortest comeback effort lasted 15 months. You may find as I did in four of the comeback churches I served that your time is short-lived. Though compelled by both brothers to stay on, the carpenter said, "I would love to stay—but I have many bridges to build." He stayed only long enough to complete the bridge. Some bridges take longer to build than others. And you may discover, as I did, that even if you want to stay on, you're not allowed to for reasons beyond your control.

In my last comeback assignment, the crisis had just ended when the opportunity came to accept a call to a church in Dallas. That church was the largest on the district. I really wanted to accept, but the timing was wrong. I had not stayed long enough to finish the bridge, so I declined the invitation. I had not yet learned to resist the temptation to second-guess myself. If you've ever wondered whether you're doing the right thing, consider the advice of a father to his son after he had just signed the closing papers on his house.

"Whatcha lookin' so glum about, boy?" he asked as he winked and slapped his son on the shoulder.

"Well, I just sold my house, and we're moving tomorrow," he replied. "Hope we're doing the right thing."

"Son, let me tell you something. You just take it from me. Don't ever look over your shoulder. And don't second-guess a major decision."[10]

Making a decision without the end in sight takes a lot of faith. Making decisions is one of the most difficult tasks a comeback pastor has to face.

Many times after turning down that large church, I thought I had made the biggest mistake of my career. Believe it or not, exactly one year later, I was appointed district superintendent of the Dallas District—and guess where my office was located. Right across the street from that same church I had turned down a year before. God wanted me in Dallas on His timetable, not my own. As Scott Walker says,

> Timing in the life of a Christian is not due to tide or chance or fate; rather, God works within our perceptions and our environments to direct the timing of opportunities and decisions that come our way. As such, God is the conductor of the symphony that is playing the score of our life. It is God who changes the tempo, directs the intensity, and works to keep all the contributing forces in harmony.[11]

Your task as a comeback pastor is to listen to the music and respond with readiness and sensitivity. I wished many times that God would show up on cue from me—just when I wanted him to. But my perception of the timing and God's perception of timing for my life and ministry were different. I've learned that God's timing is always right and that He's always on time.

What you cannot change, commit. Commit your way to the Lord.

Don't stop short by saying, "I commit, but . . ." Commitment is letting God work out the plan and the timetable. So often we want to tell God how to do what we think needs to be done. Commitment is "no strings attached." The only things that will hurt you in the comeback task are those you refuse to leave with God.

7. Build bridges that facilitate recovery.

The comeback church experience will either force you out of ministry altogether, or it will make you a survivor. To survive the experience, you must assess the situation and build a bridge. Reject any plans you might have to construct fences. Build a bridge that allows your people to release the past and cross over to a new future. Be the kind of pastor who builds bridges that facilitate recovery. Create a bond of credibility and trust with the walking wounded whom you'll surely encounter. Be authentic, real, vulnerable, honest, and truly concerned about the welfare of your people, and you will have earned the right to lead them across the bridge you built.

Physicians follow the Law of the Hippocratic Oath: "Heal, but in healing do no harm." A comeback pastor should be concerned, first and last, with doing no harm to the body of Christ or anyone in it. Terry Muck is so right to advise the leader to constantly think, "The body of Christ has a higher priority than my career; I cannot make decisions that will harm the ministry."[12] You can afford to go slow to go fast. Build bridges carefully with preparation, restraint, and fervent prayer, and you will have made a way for those who come after you. Be a good and faithful servant by giving your best effort. Never put it in neutral, coast, take it easy, or settle for average.

8. Be strong in the strength God provides.

Building bridges is tedious, tiring work. The task you face demands hard labor. This is not child's play and at times will require more of you than you have to give. But remember: the God you represent has supernatural power for your weakness as you allow Him to work through you. Looking back, if I had any success in pumping new life into deflated congregations, it was because I showed up in the power of the Spirit and allowed God to use me. I threw myself into the bridge-building process endeavoring to work smart as well as hard. I discovered the source of strength. I had to become a man of prayer. Prayer changed me, and prayer changed the churches God used me to turn around.

Prayer does not just enable us to do a greater work for God. Prayer is a greater work for God. We have a lot of power when we pray. You'll face problems that require more horsepower than you possess. God stands ready to give you what you may lack. He'll fill up what you use up. Don't blunder ahead in your own might. Keep pace with the Spirit. At times He may have to say, "Slow down," and at other times "Pick it up!" Prayer is the indispensable means by which you maintain constant communication with God. Any comeback effort will be severely limited, if not totally doomed to failure, unless you pray.

9. Learn the secret of surviving.

Only the strongest leaders survive. These are individuals with powerful, visionary leadership skills who use every ounce of strength and every shred of intellect they possess to help churches reach their comeback potential. I know I could not have survived were it not for that dirty little word—*discipline*. Becoming a successful bridge-builder requires a strong regimen of spiritual, physical, and mental discipline. A legendary football player once said, "I think guys are always curious about my regimen, but they don't want to pay the price. They don't want to feel the pain. You just have to take your body to another level; you're going to hurt."

I'm no football player, but I think I understand what he meant. To survive the comeback church experience you must pay the asking price. Discipline is what separates the men from the boys and the women from the girls. During the comeback efforts, I personally plugged into the power of prayer and involved as many church members as would accept the prayer challenge. Then I witnessed the church moving forward on its knees. I even developed some calluses of my own. Knee walking put calluses on the knees. Building bridges hardened the hands. And God was in charge of the miracles.

10. Enjoy the journey.

During all my bridge building, I had to learn to maintain balance.

The call to build bridges as a comeback pastor is unique. Since you accepted the challenge because you believed God would use you to revitalize the crisis church, enjoy the journey. God must have utmost confidence in your ability to tackle the task. So maintain your equilibrium by not taking the task or yourself too seriously. Laugh. Love. Give yourself away freely. Be a servant. Be like Jesus—fun to be around. Focus on the positive. Dare to truly connect with the people. Remember: though your church is in crisis, *you're* not in crisis. God has sent you there to help it rise to a new level.

Bridging to People

Most of us who enter ministry do so because of our great love for people. We affirm what Francis Shaeffer believed in his book *No Little People*. He argued that in God's kingdom there are no little people and no little places.[13] We know that there are small churches, but there are no unimportant members of the Body of Christ. The divine Carpenter modeled this principle well. He readily connected with people, never pursuing a selfish agenda. He freely gave himself to people in need and built bridges in broken relationships.

To build the necessary bridges in any comeback assignment, you must first connect with the people you're trying to influence. In *The 21 Most Powerful Minutes in a Leader's Day* John Maxwell writes, "The ability to connect is a quality you see in *every* great leader. No matter how much leadership talent or skill you possess, if you want to be a better leader, you must learn to connect with people effectively—not just for your own benefit, but for the benefit of your people."[14]

Connecting with the people you're trying to lead must come before anything else. Connection is the leader's responsibility and requires a lot of effort. It's believed that Bill Clinton won the 1992 United States presidential election largely because the country wanted change. His handlers also helped him stay focused on the one thing the people seemed to care most about—the economy. In their war room, Clinton's key aides put up a large banner to keep them focused on the target: "It's the economy, stupid!" Hans Finzel says leaders need a banner that reads: "It's the people, stupid!" for if we ever neglect this advice, we're the stupid ones.[15] Love is the language everyone understands. If you can't love the people you're sent to serve, you'll leave them.

At various leadership conferences I've attended, I've heard John Maxwell say repeatedly, "People don't care how much you know until they know how much you care." Task-oriented leaders would rather tackle the task than take the time to reach out to people and thus begin building the relational bridges that must be constructed. In a comeback experience, you may see so much that needs to be done that you may struggle to put and keep people before the task. People are always an interruption if task comes before people. Finzel asks, "Which comes first, person or task?" He answers, "Which is right depends on what you're doing. If you're at a party, it's people first. If you're fighting a fire, it's the task first. In the ministry of leadership, people must take priority over paper and production."[16] If a church is in crisis, you may think that instead of being a bridge-builder, you're a fireman as you frantically work to put out fires. There's a task to be accomplished, but there are people who must be brought along. This can't happen solely from behind a pulpit. You must walk among your people and connect with them one-on-one. Only when you do this are you able to effectively build the bridges that will facilitate reconciliation.

There are many bridges yet to build. May I hand you a hammer?

Notes

Chapter 1

1. Rick Warren, *The Purpose-Driven Church* (Grand Rapids: Zondervan Publishing House, 1995), 198.

Chapter 2

1. Quoted in Hans Finzel, *The Top Ten Mistakes Leaders Make* (Wheaton, Ill.: Victor Books, 1994), 31.

2. John C. Harris, *Stress, Power and Ministry* (Washington, D.C.: The Albin Institute, 1977), 59.

3. Paul Meier, *Don't Let the Jerks Get the Best of You* (Nashville: Thomas Nelson Publishers, 1993), 59.

4. Ibid., 196.

5. Warren W. Wiersbe, *On Being a Servant of God* (Grand Rapids: Baker Books, 1993), 16.

6. George Barna, *Turn-Around Churches* (Ventura, Calif.: Regal Books, 1993), 40.

7. Harold Ivan Smith, *A Decembered Grief* (Kansas City: Beacon Hill Press of Kansas City, 1999), 28.

8. Bruce Wilkerson, *The Prayer of Jabez* (Sisters, Oreg.: Multnomah Publishers, 2000), 9.

9. James M. Kouzes & Barry Z. Posner, *Credibility* (San Francisco: Jossey-Bass Publishers, 1993), 37-39.

10. George Barna, *Today's Pastors* (Ventura, Calif.: Regal Books, 1993), 49.

11. John C. Maxwell, *Developing the Leader Within You* (Nashville: Thomas Nelson Publishers, 1993), 5-11.

12. Stephen R. Covey, *The 7 Habits of Highly Effective People* (New York: Simon and Schuster, 1989), 188-90.

13. John C. Bowling, *Grace-Full Leadership* (Kansas City: Beacon Hill Press of Kansas City, 2000).

14. Finzel, *The Top Ten Mistakes Leaders Make,* 156.

15. Kouzes and Posner, *Credibility,* 90.

16. Wiersbe, *On Being a Servant of God,* 100.

Chapter Three

1. Donald E. Messer, *A Conspiracy of Goodness,* cited in Rueben P. Job, *A Guide To Retreat for All God's Shepherds* (Nashville: Abingdon Press, 1994), 162.

2. Vernon C. Grounds, "Still the World's Greatest Job!" *Ministry,* September 1999, 10-13.

3. Richard Blackmow, cited in H. B. London Jr., "The Weekly Pastor's Briefing," *Focus on the Family* 7:7 (February 12, 1999), 1.

Chapter Four

1. C. Peter Wagner, *The Healthy Church* (Ventura, Calif.: Regal Books, 1996), 43-55.

2. Ibid., 45.

3. Wiersbe, *On Being a Servant of God*, 70.

4. Quoted in Dave Ray, *Wake Up! You Have a Ministry!* (Central, Mich.: Core Ministries, 2000), 10.

5. Kennon L. Callahan, "The New Reality in Motivation," *Leadership*, fall 1999, 32.

Chapter Five

1. H. B. London Jr., "Facts Are Facts," in "The Pastor's Weekly Briefing, *Focus on the Family* 7:35 (August 27, 1999), 1.

2. Frances Meeker, *Nashville Banner*, June 2, 1995, B-1.

3. H. B. London Jr. and Neil B. Wiseman, *Pastors at Risk* (Wheaton, Ill.: Victor Books, 1993), 30.

4. Ibid., 46.

5. John Schmidt, "Putting Them in Their Place," on web site of Pastoral Advocacy Center, January 23, 2001, <http://www.gardenministries.com>. The site addresses this problem and intends to pose solutions to the forced termination of pastors.

6. London and Wiseman, *Pastors at Risk*, 47.

7. Schmidt, "Putting Them in Their Place."

8. John C. Maxwell, *The 21 Most Powerful Minutes in a Leader's Day* (Nashville: Thomas Nelson Publishers, 2000), 104.

9. Wilkerson, *The Prayer of Jabez*, 9.

10. John C. Maxwell, *Developing the Leader Within You*, 42.

11. Neil T. Anderson and Charles Mylander, *Setting Your Church Free* (Ventura, Calif.: Regal Books, 1994), 73.

12. Finzel *The Top Ten Mistakes Leaders Make*, 136.

13. Covey, *The 7 Habits of Highly Effective People*, 188-202.

Chapter Six

1. Quoted in Ray, *Wake Up! You Have a Ministry!* 30.

2. Ibid., 28-29.

3. Will Eva, "It's Worth Dying For," *Ministry*, November 2000, 4.

Chapter Seven

1. Cited in H. B. London Jr., "The Weekly Pastor's Briefing," *Focus on the Family* 7:7 (February 12, 1999), 1.

2. Livingstone Rasalam, "The Vicious Cycle," January 23, 2001, <http://www.rasalam.com/ministries>.

3. Norman Moore, "Let's Encourage Our Pastor and Spouse," unpublished. Used by permission.

4. Quoted in Marshall Shelley, editorial, *Leadership*, fall 2000, 3.

5. Shepherd Care web site: <http://shepherdcare.com>.

6. John Schmidt, "Putting Them in Their Place," January 23, 2001, <www.gardenministries.com>.

7. Cal and Rose Samra, *Holy Humor* (New York: Master Media Limited, 1996), 135.

8. Barna, *Today's Pastors*, 52.

9. London, "The Weekly Pastor's Briefing," *Focus on the Family* 7:7, 1.

10. Quoted in Alan Heller, "Not-So-Great Expectations," *Focus on the Family* 25:2 (February 2001), 14.

11. Moore, "Let's Encourage Our Pastor and Spouse."

12. London and Wiseman, *Pastors at Risk*, 41.

13. Moore, "Let's Encourage Our Pastor and Spouse."

14. London and Wiseman, *Pastors at Risk*, 61.

15. Schmidt, "Putting Them in Their Place."

16. Ibid.

17. Moore, "Let's Encourage Our Pastor and Spouse."

18. Dennis Rainey, *Pulling Weeds, Planting Seeds* (San Bernardino, Calif.: Here's Life Publishers, 1989) 53.

19. John Stott, *The Contemporary Christian* (Downer's Grove, Ill.: InterVarsity Press, 1992), 112.

20. Ibid.

21. Victor M. Parachin, "Dealing with Criticism," *Ministry*, September 2001, 16.

22. Gordon MacDonald, *Restoring Your Spiritual Passion* (Nashville: Oliver Nelson, 1986), 105.

23. London, "The Pastor's Weekly Briefing," *Focus on the Family* 7:7, 1.

24. Vance Havner, *Hearts Afire* (Old Tappan: Fleming H. Revell, 1952), 22.

25. London and Wiseman, *Pastors at Risk*, 36.

26. Moore, "Let's Encourage our Pastor and Spouse."

27. MacDonald, *Restoring Your Spiritual Passion,* 87.

28. Quoted in Wiersbe, *On Being a Servant of God*, 17.

Chapter Eight

1. Steven L. Burns, "How to Survive Unbearable Stress," www.teachhealth.com.

2. Joe McKeever, "Broken Pastor, Broken Church," *Leadership,* winter 2001, 60.

3. Jay Kessler, *Raising Responsible Kids* (Brentwood, Tenn.: Wolgemuth & Hyatt, 1991), 15.

4. Charles L. Allen, *God's Psychiatry* (Grand Rapids: Fleming H. Revell Co., 1953), 70.

5. Bill Hybels, *Honest to God?* (Grand Rapids: Zondervan Books, 1990), 53-56.

6. Gary Rosberg, *Guard Your Heart* (Sisters, Oreg.: Multnomah Press, 1994), 119-20.

7. C. Peter Wagner, *The Prayer Shield* (Ventura, Calif.: Regal Books, 1992), 73.

8. Ibid., 66.

9. H. B. London Jr., "Standing Firm," *Focus on the Family* 25:2, February 2001, 15.

10. "Pastors Viewing Internet Pornography," The Leadership Survey, *Leadership* 22:1 (winter 2001), 89.

11. Warren W. Wiersbe, *The Integrity Crisis* (Nashville: Oliver Nelson, 1988), 17-18.

12. Quoted in Alan E. Nelson, *Broken in the Right Place* (Nashville: Thomas Nelson Publishers, 1994), 220.

13. Stanley J. Grentz and Roy D. Bell, "Predator, Wanderer, or Lover," *Leadership 16:3* (summer 1995), 36.

14. Rosberg, *Guard Your Heart,* 120.

15. "Pastors Viewing Internet Pornography," 89.

16. Eric Reed, "Hooked," *Leadership,* winter 2001, 86-94.

17. James Dobson, "Focus on the Family" radio broadcast, date unknown.

Chapter Nine

1. Barna, *Turn-Around Churches*, 22.

2. Scott Walker, *Life-Rails* (Philadelphia: Westminster Press, 1987), 71-72.

3. Quoted in Terry Muck, *When to Take a Risk* (Waco, Tex.: Christianity Today and Word, 1987), 95.

4. Maxwell, *Developing the Leader Within You*, 171.

5. Finzel, *The Top Ten Mistakes Leaders Make*, 111.

6. Garry Wills, *Certain Trumpets* (New York: Simon and Schuster, 1994), 13.

7. Ibid., 17

8. Alan E. Nelson, *Broken in the Right Place* (Nashville: Thomas Nelson Publishers), 14.

9. Ibid., 122.

10. Walker, *Life-Rails,* 86.

11. Ibid., 80-81.

12. Muck, *When to Take a Risk*, 102.

13. Quoted in Finzel, *The Top Ten Mistakes Leaders Make,* 129.

14. Maxwell, *The 21 Most Powerful Minutes in a Leader's Day*, 156.

15. Finzel, *The Top Ten Mistakes Leaders Make,* 50.

16. Ibid., 49.